The Golden Hawks of Genghis Khan

BY RITA RITCHIE
author of "The Year of the Horse"

Illustrated by Lorence F. Bjorklund

NEW YORK
E. P. DUTTON & CO., INC.

To

IRMA REITCI

who began it all.

Copyright, ©, 1958 by E. P. Dutton & Co., Inc.
All rights reserved. Printed in the U. S. A.

¶ *No part of this book may be reproduced in any form without permission in writing from the publisher, except by a reviewer who wishes to quote brief passages in connection with a review written for inclusion in magazine or newspaper or radio broadcast.*

Contents

1	The House of Kurush	7
2	The Stranger from Urgendj	15
3	Flight from Samarkand	27
4	A Bow Is Drawn	41
5	A Horn of Trouble	55
6	The City of Genghis Khan	69
7	Master of the Golden Hawks	81
8	Who Is Torgul?	94
9	A Prize for the Hawker	107
10	Talons for Revenge	119
11	The Shadow of the Kang	132
12	Escape from Karakorum	141
13	Wasteland	152
14	The Beat of Wings	164
15	Torgul Returns	176
	Bibliography	189

1   The House of Kurush

Jalair opened his eyes to the midmorning sun flooding into his room. In no hurry to arise, he stretched lazily, enjoying the luxury of sleeping late now that he was home from school for the summer.

Through the open window, he studied the clear blue sky beyond the high stone wall surrounding his grandfather's house, and he could just see the treetops of the parks that circled Samarkand.

Puzzled, he frowned. Already the trading season had begun, yet the sky above the parks was strangely empty.

Then his heart leaped, for a hawk shot up clear of the trees. From its color and markings, Jalair knew it for a kestrel.

The hawk ringed upward, the sun flashing on its brown back and slate-gray wings. The kestrel reached its pitch, and hung in the sky. Jalair knew what it was waiting for.

Often visitors to Samarkand, impatient with the hours it took for a caravan to be made up, would gather in the parks to match their hawks' performance. The master of the kestrel would soon start swinging the padded and feathered lure.

There!

The kestrel's keen eyes must have caught the circling lure, for it suddenly snapped its wings flat to its sleek body and plunged down and down, head foremost. The hawk's stoop took it out of Jalair's view, but he knew that at the last instant, the kestrel would swing upward and, with closed talons, deal a mighty blow to its mock prey.

Jalair leaned against the sill of the open window, thinking of past summers when his grandfather Kurush allowed him to ride his pony beyond the walls of the house. He always directed Cephas, his ever-present servant and bodyguard, toward the parks to see the hawkers and their birds. He would watch them breathlessly, dreaming of slipping the Golden Hawk from his fist while the other men gasped in astonishment at the finest hawk in the world.

Suddenly Jalair pulled on his clothes. How could he possibly have forgotten that this was a special day? He laughed at himself as he slipped into his white outer tunic, belted it at his waist, and stepped into his sandals.

Cephas, in a long white robe and plain turban, entered Jalair's room with a bowl of water. "What, up already, young master? The boat bringing you home from Guzar arrived so late last night that Master Kurush said you might sleep your fill."

Jalair laughed again, thinking of at last joining the hawkers in the parks. "Cephas, do you remember what day this is?"

"Your first in Samarkand this summer," the servant replied. He went to the bundles on a low shelf and began unpacking Jalair's things.

"It is the day I go to Eli the Levantine's, to select the pair of hawks Kurush promised last year to buy for me." He washed his face at the bowl Cephas had brought, then rubbed vigorously with a towel the servant handed him. "What kind shall I get, Cephas?"

The servant sorted and folded Jalair's winter clothes, setting some aside to be mended. "I know nothing of hawks, young master. But surely you have decided after thinking of them for a year."

"For years and years," Jalair corrected. "The peregrine is best, but hardest to train." He sat on his bed and watched the unpacking. "What made Kurush change his mind about the hawks?"

Cephas shook his head. "I know not, young master. But your grandfather may have wearied of your constant efforts to persuade him. Perhaps this is his way of keeping you from idling with men in the street at Eli the Levantine's. In truth, such conduct is not becoming of the grandson of the Treasurer's Steward of Samarkand. Some day you may rise to a position in the city government, Jalair, and you must be a gentleman."

"But Eli is my friend," Jalair protested. "And so are the men who buy their hawks from him."

Cephas nodded. "I have seen the happy hours you spent with them while I held our mounts. Yet your grandfather Kurush wishes you to be careful in selecting your companions."

"I know," Jalair said shortly. "That is why he sends me to Guzar."

Guzar was a tiny village tucked away in the hills high

above the great Oxus River Valley. Its people lived by fishing and a little farming. The few boys Jalair's own age worked from dawn to dusk, sowing and reaping, or helping pull in the nets and clean the fish. For his only companion, Jalair had Sayyid Hussayn, with whom he lived and studied most of the year in a small mosque much in need of repair. After the day's schoolwork was done, they went for walks, and in the evening played chess. The school year was long and tiresome, but at least Jalair was not continually watched by Kurush, whose anger was so easily aroused.

But now he would have his long-awaited hawks, and he could take them back to Guzar. Sayyid Hussayn had promised to give him a storeroom in one of the little-used minarets to turn into a hawk mews.

"Jalair!" Cephas said sharply. "What have you done?"

Startled, he turned toward Cephas, and saw in the servant's hand a small plaque Jalair had carved during the school year. In low relief was a hawk plunging earthward to its sighted prey, every detail carefully carved. Beneath it was chiseled the jagged line of a thunderbolt.

"You know this is forbidden," Cephas warned.

"I know," Jalair said, his throat suddenly dry.

Where the design had come from and what it meant, Jalair could not tell. It was a picture that had been in his mind all his life. He called it the Golden Hawk, in honor of the real Golden Hawks he had never seen, though he was determined to recover the strain some day.

"You will not show it to Kurush, will you?" he asked Cephas apprehensively. Twice before in past years Kurush had found Jalair making that design.

"Yes, he will show it to me," commanded a stern voice.

Jalair whirled.

Kurush was standing in the doorway. He held out his hand. "Give it to me, Cephas." The servant did so. "Go to the kitchen, Cephas," Kurush ordered. "See that Jalair's breakfast is made ready."

The servant quickly slipped away.

"The design I forbade you to make," Kurush mused, looking at the carved plaque in his hand. His face darkened and his chest expanded, making his gold-embroidered silken robe rustle with the coming anger. The sapphire in his turban winked like an all-knowing eye.

"I—I carved it at Guzar, to make the evenings go faster." But Jalair knew explanations were useless.

"And you brought it here to insult me with your disobedience?" Kurush moved closer, his richly decorated velvet slippers silent on the stone floor.

"Truly, I did not mean to bring it," Jalair said. "It was in a box I was going to leave behind, but Sayyid Hussayn's servant must have packed it with my things."

"Did Sayyid Hussayn admire your handiwork?" Kurush asked in a biting tone.

"I did not let him see it," Jalair answered. "Nor has anyone seen it but you and Cephas." He had kept this plaque hidden, for the Moslem religion forbade depicting any living form.

"It was very wrong for you to do this, Jalair," Kurush said sternly. "I thought my previous punishments had made you forget the design. Perhaps I should use stronger methods."

Jalair thought at once of the hawks for which he had pleaded these many years. "Don't take my hawks away from me, Grandfather! I only made the plaque because I was thinking of them, and when I have real hawks I will not make the design any more."

"You have not only disobeyed the Prophet," Kurush thundered, snapping the wood in his hands, "but you disobeyed me! You are only a boy, Jalair, and there are many things you do not understand."

"I will never do it again," Jalair promised. "For now I will have real hawks instead of wooden ones."

"The only reason I am not going to punish you," Kurush said, his hand still closed hard over the fragments of wood, "is that you must be your best in front of the visitor who comes this evening."

"Then I may have the hawks?" Jalair asked, almost fearing the answer. Kurush grunted assent. "May I go to Eli the Levantine's and select the pair today?"

"If Cephas is not too busy to accompany you. And you

must return in time for the evening meal. A man from Urgendj will dine with us."

Relieved, Jalair stepped to the doorway.

"One moment," Kurush commanded. "You are back in Samarkand, and you must be careful."

Jalair sighed impatiently, knowing by heart the warnings Kurush always recited when he returned from Guzar. He waited, hardly listening to his grandfather's voice.

"You must never go out without Cephas, and while with him, obey his every word. You must never, never tell anyone who your parents were. I know it is hard for you not to boast of your father, Darien, and the Golden Hawk strain he created, but word easily goes from mouth to mouth. It flies down the caravan trails, it travels to the ears of the Mongols in the land of Genghis Khan. And then, Jalair, if you are not careful, the Mongols will come to slay you. Once before you escaped their swords, and they never suffer anyone to do that and live."

It seemed to Jalair that this time the yearly warning was worded more strongly than usual, but, anxious to escape from Kurush, he said nothing. After all, was he not safe in Samarkand, in the heart of the great empire of Khoresm? Surely no Mongols would dare risk their strength against Shah Ala-u-Din's mighty armies!

Cephas was just setting Jalair's breakfast on the rough wooden table when he entered the kitchen. "Will you still have your hawks, young master?" Cephas asked in genuine concern.

"Yes," Jalair answered, hastily eating his stewed fruit. "Kurush said I must look my best for someone coming to dine with us tonight. Who is it?"

"A stranger from Urgendj," Cephas said. "More I know not, but surely he must have a high position from all the orders Kurush has given for tonight's feast."

"From Shah Ala-u-Din's court?" Jalair asked, for Urgendj was the capital city.

"Perhaps, for this banquet is to be finer than that we prepared when Samarkand's governor consented to dine at the house of Kurush."

"I am glad Grandfather is in a good mood," Jalair said, "or I would not have my hawks. Can we go to the market place now, Cephas?"

The servant shook his head. "I am sorry, young master. But there is so much work for the other servants that I must help."

"But Cephas, I must see my hawks today!"

During the long journey downriver from Guzar he had been able to think of nothing but his hawks. And when he had seen the walls and watchtowers of Samarkand outlined with flickering torches just before the boat docked, Jalair had nearly burst with yearning to go at once to Eli's.

"Perhaps there would be no harm if you went alone," Cephas suggested cautiously, cutting a big slice of cold lamb for Jalair's breakfast. Occasionally in the past Cephas had permitted Jalair to go off by himself. "I will be busy in the kitchen and stables all day," he said. "Kurush will not miss you, but promise me you will be cautious, young master."

Jalair finished his breakfast and rose eagerly. "I will return for the evening meal," he promised. "I wish I could ride Rustum to the market place."

Cephas shook his head firmly. "You must walk if you are to go alone. Here is your spending money."

Jalair took the leather bag of coins Kurush had set aside for him. He walked through the kitchen garden with its playing fountain, passed through a gate in an inner wall, and entered the stable. Kurush owned many fine horses—blooded Persians—but Jalair passed them without a glance and went directly to his fat little pony.

Rustum was happy to see his young master, and nuzzled against his shoulder. Jalair patted his nose and promised they would soon go for a ride.

"I am going to select my hawks, Rustum," he told the pony. "Tomorrow Kurush will go with me to buy them. And then you and I will gallop beneath them while they circle in the sky. But you must be patient, for I will have to train them first."

Giving Rustum a final pat on the nose, Jalair went out into the stable courtyard where a fountain spun three silvery streams into the air. He walked toward the great wrought-iron gates set in the outer wall, then stopped short in surprise.

A strange horseman had stopped to stare inside the iron gates. His gaze shifted to Jalair.

The boy stared back, matching the rider's open curiosity. This was the oddest man Jalair had ever seen in his life. Yet, somehow, Jalair knew they had met before, if only in a wild dream.

The rider was dressed in long baggy trousers of wool tucked into rich black leather boots with upturned toes. He had on a thick jacket, belted with great links of silver, and above his waist on the rider's left showed the jeweled haft of a sword. His head was covered with a peaked wool cap, the earflaps folded up because of Samarkand's heat. On his chest, hung by a chain around his neck, was a polished tablet of copper bearing the beaten design of a tiger. Jalair noted the bronze face with its long black mustache, and the muscular hands gripping the reins. The rider sat his horse well, but with a bearing that was proud and haughty.

The horseman and the boy stared at each other boldly.

This, Jalair thought, was a horseman out of the secret land.

Jalair often slipped into a strange reverie of a wonderful land, where the mountains were higher than the hills surrounding Guzar, where rivers stormed down rocky canyons and foamed with rage. It was a land where the wind was strong and as cold as ice, where broad plains stretching as far as the eye could see were scented with grass half as tall as a man. And Jalair pictured bold horsemen shouting and laughing as they galloped on swift and hardy mounts.

Somehow this dream land was connected with the Golden Hawk and the picture Jalair was forbidden to make, but he could not understand how these things fitted together. It was no use to ask Kurush.

The rider and Jalair stared at each other for a long minute, while the wild thoughts of grassy plains dashed through the boy's mind. And then with a casual flick of his reins, the horseman was gone.

Jalair ran back to the kitchen. Finding it empty, he went

to the storeroom where Cephas was helping the cook. The servant looked at Jalair, then went out to the garden with him. "What is it, Jalair?"

"The horseman," Jalair said. "Who is he, and where does he come from?" He described the man at the stable gate, and Cephas' face became serious.

"Jalair," the servant said, "perhaps you should stay in the house today."

"But who was that man? Why did he stare at me?"

Cephas hesitated. "That man was a Mongol."

Anger grew in Jalair's heart that the dream of the secret land should be thus spoiled. Then the hatred dissolved into a sickening fear.

"Cephas!" Jalair cried. "Have the Mongols come for me?"

2 The Stranger from Urgendj

The green and gold silence of the garden was broken only by the soft pattering of the fountain.

Samarkand—the scented city of groves and pleasure gardens, of flowers and fruits, a city of busy trade that paused five times a day to answer the summons to prayer.

And now there were Mongols in the streets.

"Have they come for me?" Jalair repeated fearfully.

"No, no, young master!" Cephas hastened to reassure him. "There is no one in Samarkand or even in Guzar who could ever lead them to you. Now you see why Kurush has shielded you from friendships that might turn into treachery."

Jalair stared into the stable courtyard and the gates that barred it from the street.

Cephas read his thoughts. "That horseman was only curious about the fine house and gardens of Kurush. He knows not the boy who stared back at him."

"They killed my father and stole the Golden Hawks," Jalair said bitterly. "What are thieves and murderers doing in Khoresm?"

"Last summer, Shah Ala-u-Din signed a trade treaty with their ruler, Genghis Khan," Cephas explained. "In the fall, after you went to Guzar, the Mongols began sending trade caravans to Samarkand and other large Khoresmian cities. They stopped coming only in the worst of the winter, and began trading again early this spring, even though the mountain passes were still frozen."

"I thought our Shah was a just man," Jalair muttered. "How can he desire trade with savages?"

"Hush, Jalair," Cephas cautioned. "You must never speak against the Shah, for your grandfather hopes some day to rise from the governor's court to the palace of Shah Ala-u-Din in Urgendj. And remember, Jalair, conqueror though Genghis Khan is, he is master of Cathay and has reopened the caravan route to the far east. The Khoresmian empire has need of Cathayan goods."

"I think it is a trick," Jalair replied. "These Mongols are nothing but spies."

"The Shah's army is invincible," Cephas reminded him. "But though your hatred of the Mongols is a just one, your enmity may bring their attention upon you. For this reason, perhaps you should remain at home today."

"I am not afraid of Mongols," Jalair declared boldly. "Let me go to Eli's, Cephas. I promise to keep away from those savages." But in his heart he longed to cry insults at the eastern traders.

Cephas frowned thoughtfully. "Very well, but do not linger, even though the hawkers draw you into conversation. Return quickly."

The memory of the arrogant horseman at the gates was still vivid, so Jalair left the grounds by a small foot-gate near the kitchen. At first he turned toward the nearest of the parks where the hawkers were flinging their hunters into the sky. But thinking he might meet other Mongols, Jalair decided to go directly through the city itself.

It was a long way from the spacious houses of the residential section to the narrow winding business streets. Yet the thought of the hawks soon to be his quickened Jalair's footsteps. His pace slowed when he neared the great square where caravans were often formed, for the streets were crowded with wandering peddlers, water-carriers, beggars, errand boys, story-tellers entertaining their audiences, and veiled women examining shop goods as their servants hovered respectfully behind them.

The square was further crowded by a caravan forming its train. Jalair slipped through a maze of people and animals to the fountain in the center. Careful not to soil his sandals in the mud around the base of the fountain, he cupped his hands and drank deeply of the cold water.

Then he pushed his way through the camels, oxen, horses, and carts of the caravan, and came to Eli the Levantine's hawk shop.

Through the open half of the stall, he saw Eli busy inside, tying newly arrived hawks to their perches along the walls. "Jalair!" cried the merchant warmly when he caught sight of him. "Come in. How did the school year pass?"

"How are you, Eli?" Jalair returned, stepping through the

doorway. "School went as usual. May I help you with the new hawks?"

"I am almost finished," the merchant replied. "But look at these birds! I will not sell a one. See, the Europeans refuse to use the leather hood as we do."

Jalair bent close, and saw that each bird had the upper lid fastened to the lower by a tiny loop of thread. The Europeans called this "seeling," and though it was necessary to keep untrained hawks sightless, Jalair thought seeling was a cruel practice. He knew too that a hawk could be better trained if the leather hood were used. "Where did you get these hawks?"

"They came from Salerno, and I took them only because the merchant owes me money and cannot pay." Eli turned to a shelf and brought down a small wooden box. "But see what I have saved for you, Jalair! The hawkers heard you were at last getting a pair of hawks, and all year they kept bringing these things for you."

"Equipment for the mews!" Jalair exclaimed, excitedly exploring through the box. There were leashes and jesses, metal rings and leather straps that had a dozen uses, several kinds of leather hoods, and bells to be tied to the feet of the hawks. Jalair pulled on the leather gauntlet and decided that with a little fixing it would fit his hand. "And bow perches!" he said, picking up the small curved perches whose sharpened points could be pushed into the ground.

"The hawker who comes from Chirakchi promised to bring two weathering blocks this summer," Eli told him. "And I shall give you some falcon socks to take along with your birds today."

"It is tomorrow that I will fetch my hawks," Jalair said. "First I must select the ones I wish and tell Kurush their price. May I pick them out now?"

Eli nodded, and went to attend to a customer while Jalair slowly walked along the rows of tethered hawks. Quickly he passed up the lesser breeds, paused longingly in front of a magnificent white Nordic gyrfalcon, then gravely examined the remaining hawks.

He thought of all the advice the hawkers had given him,

and remembered their conversations among themselves. Though he longed for a pair of the better strains, he knew he had not the experience to train them. Then too, the wooded hills of Guzar eliminated the higher soaring breeds.

At last his choice narrowed to two pairs of goshawks. Though not high flyers as hawks go, they worked well in forested country.

Carefully he examined the beaks, talons, and flight feathers, and finally settled on a fine pair whose claws promised great seizing power. He liked their stiff feathers that gleamed even in the faint light of the shop, and their strongly formed beaks.

"Have you chosen?" Eli asked, coming close.

"Yes. This pair."

"You have a fine eye for hawks," Eli smiled.

"Eli, will you be sure not to sell them before tomorrow?" Now that Jalair had chosen the hawks, he felt no others could be his own but these.

"They will be here tomorrow," Eli promised.

"And I will take my mews equipment home when Kurush and I come for the hawks," Jalair said. He was about to leave Eli's shop when he noticed a man enter. He was dressed in clothes similar to those Jalair had seen on the Mongol horseman at the stable gates.

This Mongol's short thick jacket was open because of the heat, and Jalair saw that it was lined with fur. Instead of a cap, he wore a leather helmet bound with iron straps, and from it fell a white horsetail crest. Heavy gloves were thrust into the man's wide leather belt which was richly decorated with silver and gold. A short curved sword hung carelessly at his side, but from its worn hilt, Jalair knew the Mongol was accustomed to wielding the weapon.

He swallowed his anger and fear, remembering his promise to Cephas. But then he saw that the Mongol was making very free with Eli's hawks. He even untied them from their perches and felt their bones and muscles. He went as far as unhooding them to feel the shape of the head.

Eli never allowed anyone to touch the hawks, but he was busy with two other men, Khoresmians, and probably did not notice the Mongol. Jalair waited until Eli was free, then pointed to the Mongol. "He might ruin your hawks if you do not stop him," he warned in a low voice.

The merchant looked up, then hastily glanced away. "Quiet, Jalair. Let him alone."

"Do you let savages abuse your birds?" Jalair demanded angrily.

"I beg of you, do not let him hear you," Eli cautioned. "He is a Mongol, the leader of the caravan making up in the square. We must let these people have their own way. They are honest traders, but allow no interference when they come to buy. A Mongol can become very angry indeed." Then his voice softened. "He will not hurt the hawks, Jalair. I have seen Mongols handle the birds with an expert touch."

Jalair stalked out of the shop, hurt and angry that Eli had defended the Mongol. At the fountain in the square he plunged his hands in the cold water, cooling the wrists that throbbed with wrath.

Glancing at the caravan that was forming nearby, he saw other men dressed in the Mongol fashion. They walked about, filled greatly with their own importance as they assigned places in the train to merchants who were Khoresmian, Persian, Arabic, and Syrian. Jalair viewed these merchants with contempt as they spoke respectfully to the Mongols. If he were a trader, he would rather take the risk of traveling alone than put himself under Mongol protection!

Just then Jalair caught a movement he had feared since he left Eli's shop. The Mongol inside was reaching for Jalair's own goshawks! He handled them freely and seemed pleased with them. Jalair's heart thudded wildly. Eli was frightened enough of the Mongols to break his promise to Jalair and sell the goshawks. Jalair glanced around wildly, seeking some means to stop the Mongol from taking his hawks away.

Then he noticed once more the mud around the base of the fountain where water-carriers had splashed in filling their jars. Jalair scooped up a handful, and with an accuracy born of desperation, threw it across the street, straight into the open shop. The mud ball spattered on the back of the Mongol's head. The man whirled, crying out angrily, his hand drawing his sword.

Jalair did not wait to see any more. He dashed off through the street and dodged down a narrow alleyway. He could hear other shouts, the lowing of frightened oxen, and booted feet pounding after him as the Mongols in the square took up the chase.

Twisting and turning, Jalair slipped through every short cut and hideaway he knew. The market place gave way to quieter streets. The shouts and footsteps were far behind, but Jalair ran on past schools, mosques, and fine houses until he came to the parks under the city walls.

He threw himself down at the edge of a pond, and gradually regained his breath.

The insult to the Mongol was little enough, yet it was a blow at the dreaded warriors who had taken from Jalair both parents, and the Golden Hawks. His father, Darien, would have been pleased at his gesture of defiance.

He wished he could remember what his parents looked like, for when that terrible thing happened he was only a small boy. Kurush had told him the story so often that Jalair knew it well.

Irian, Kurush's only child, had been the most beautiful woman in all Khoresm, even lovelier than the women in the Persian part of the empire. Darien had been tall and strong, and the greatest hawker in the country.

They lived at Shah Ala-u-Din's court in Urgendj, and there Jalair had been born. Darien was Hawker to the Shah, and he worked hard for years to create a strain of magnificent hawks in the ruler's honor. He succeeded, and called the splendid new breed the Golden Hawk.

Before the new Goldens could even be trained for hunting, Darien was sent east to capture a kind of hawk of which the Shah had heard. And so Darien, Irian, and four-year-old Jalair journeyed east beyond the great mountains and around a huge desert. The Golden Hawks went also, for the breed was so new and the number of hawks so small that Darien feared to put them in another's care.

When the small hawk-seeking caravan was near the border of Cathay, so said Kurush, a band of Mongols swept out of the north and fell upon them.

Kurush's words came back to Jalair. "The Mongols slew your father and almost all of the caravan attendants. They stole the precious Golden Hawks, and they kidnaped your mother. But a servant on a swift horse snatched you up from the cart where you lay, and escaped back to Samarkand. Later," Kurush always added, "I received word from some traders who had passed through the land of Genghis Khan. Irian, your mother, had been made a slave, and within a year she died of the harsh treatment. But from her the Mongols learned the name of the child who escaped, and they vowed to track you down."

And so Jalair came to live in the house of Kurush, though he could not remember a time when he had not been under his grandfather's roof. The servant who rescued him had soon died of arrow wounds he received during the flight. This saddened Jalair, for he had many questions, and Kurush was not one to talk freely.

Idly Jalair traced his favorite design in the soft dirt beside the pool—the picture of the hawk plunging, and, beneath it, the lightning bolt. The Golden Hawk. Some day, when he was grown, he would recover the Golden Hawks from the plundering Mongols, and bring them back to the court of Shah Ala-u-Din.

It was long past noon, and Jalair's stomach reminded him he had not eaten. He rubbed out the design that always angered Kurush, then sought out a little shop nearby. A skewer of roasted lamb, some raisins, and two fresh rolls were his lunch, washed down with pomegranate juice. Then he returned to the parks.

The sky was empty of hawks, nor did he meet any hawkers in his wandering through the groves that circled the city. He wanted to go back to Eli's shop to make certain his hawks were still there. But he dared not. Eli might have seen him throw the mud, and perhaps this hasty action had caused harm to fall upon his merchant friend. Yet it had been the only way to stop the Mongol from taking his goshawks. It was enough those savages had stolen the Golden Hawks.

The sun gradually changed from the hard color of brass to the soft sheen of beaten copper as it sank toward the west. The evening breeze was heavy with the sweet scent of flowers, and shadows grew long and lazy. Over the city, from slender tiled minarets, drifted the echoing calls of the muezzins.

Jalair would be late for dinner. He left the circle of parks and slipped through the evening crowds. The market place was empty of the caravan that had filled it that morning. Eli the Levantine had closed his shop, but it was the usual hour for him to lock up. Jalair walked quickly through the city to the house of Kurush.

Cephas was in the hallway when Jalair entered the house. "You are late, young master," he said with a frown. "Dinner is already finished. Go into the kitchen for your meal, then see your grandfather at once. He knows you went without me."

"Is he angry, Cephas?"

"He made light of your absence at dinner," the servant replied. "The stranger from Urgendj wears fine clothes, and Kurush seeks to make a good impression upon him. No, we do not even know the visitor's name, for Kurush has acted with great secrecy."

Jalair ate quickly the cold fowl that had been set aside for him, then ran to his room to wash and change into a fresh tunic of white silk. Impatiently he wound around his head the long silk cloth that formed his turban, another concession to important visitors. He dropped his grass-stained clothes in a corner, along with his muddy sandals. In velvet slippers he padded swiftly through the spacious rooms, and out to the inner garden where Kurush sat playing chess with the stranger.

His grandfather had on his richest turban, the one with the big emerald set in the front. The green stone went well with Kurush's embroidered robes. The stranger from Urgendj, true to Cephas' words, had on fine garments of rainbow-colored silk, and slippers woven from strands of gold and silver. His turban bore a ruby that dwarfed Kurush's large emerald.

"Here is the boy now," Kurush said, glancing up as Jalair approached. Kurush's usually stern face was creased with an unaccustomed smile. "Will you take coffee with us, Jalair?"

Startled, Jalair could only nod. Just once before in his life had he been privileged to drink the expensive beverage.

Kurush clapped his hands and servants glided forth. He gave a series of orders, and instantly steaming thick coffee was set on a table that had been brought, and rich cream was added. A fire was kindled in a brass bowl to lighten the gloom of evening. Finally a tray of candies was passed around.

"Have you had a good walk, Jalair?" Kurush asked. He added to the stranger, "You must forgive the boy for missing his dinner. But he has not seen Samarkand since last fall."

"Samarkand will seem as nothing when he sees the great city of Urgendj," the stranger smiled. "Would you like to go there, Jalair?"

"Am I to visit Urgendj?" Jalair asked, surprised.

"Perhaps. Now, Jalair, what have you learned in school?" the stranger asked.

So the man was a scholar! And Kurush must have brought him here to see if Sayyid Hussayn in Guzar was doing his work well.

"I began the study of algebra this year," Jalair said. "And continued my work in history and geography. Sayyid Hussayn says I speak Arabic well now. And I studied Persian for two years. I also did compositions in my own language, Turki."

The stranger nodded in satisfaction and then asked many questions about mathematics, poetry, history, and the Koran. At last he leaned back in his chair. "The boy has learned well."

Kurush seemed immensely pleased.

Suddenly the stranger asked a question that took Jalair by surprise. "Do you like Mongols, Jalair?"

"I hate them!" he blurted. Then he remembered Cephas' words of caution that morning. He must not speak against Shah Ala-u-Din's trade treaty.

"It is not wise to show hatred for a powerful neighbor," the stranger said gently. "Do you not know they have conquered Cathay?"

"They rule with terror and injustice," Jalair said. "Shah Ala-u-Din is greater than their Genghis Khan, because the Shah rules with kindness."

The stranger smiled. To Kurush he said, "You have reared him rightly. Tomorrow, we will go to Urgendj."

Tomorrow! "But we are to buy my hawks tomorrow," Jalair protested. "Can we put off this visit?"

"It is not a visit, Jalair," Kurush said. "You are to live at the court of Shah Ala-u-Din. They will give you a finer teacher than even Sayyid Hussayn."

"Am I not to return to Guzar?" Jalair asked anxiously. Sayyid Hussayn had already promised him space for his hawks.

"No," Kurush said. "I will write a letter to Sayyid Hussayn, telling him you will not return this fall."

"Come, be of cheer!" the stranger encouraged. "You will live in the palace. You will learn the arts of graceful life, such as chess, polo, poetry recitation, and the soft speech of diplomats. If you study hard, the Shah will give you an important position when you are grown."

Hope stirred in Jalair's heart. "Am I to become Hawker to the Shah, as was my father?"

Both men laughed, making Jalair feel foolish.

"There are greater things planned for you," Kurush said.

"You might become an ambassador to foreign lands," the stranger added. "Someday you will even employ a hawker of your own. But enough of future dreams. Jalair, you must be ready to leave with me early tomorrow morning."

"But the hawks," Jalair said. "We must buy them tomorrow, so I can take them to court with me."

"The boy seems deeply concerned with hawking." The stranger frowned.

"It is but a passing fancy," Kurush answered impatiently. "Once he enters the life of the court, he will soon forget this foolishness."

"What is wrong with hawking?" Jalair demanded, forgetting his manners in his concern. "My father was the greatest hawker in the empire. He created the Golden Hawk strain in honor of the Shah."

During the embarrassed silence, the stranger looked at Kurush. There was a trace of suspicion in the glance.

"Your father, Darien, hoped that his son would rise to a higher position in life," Kurush said firmly. "He did not intend that his son should hold the menial position of hawker. This is not work for a gentleman." His usual severe frown came back. "The matter is settled, Jalair."

"May I at least take my hawks to Urgendj?" Jalair asked in desperation.

"Enough!" cried Kurush. "Forget the hawks. Now go to your room. You must rise early for the journey."

With a sinking heart Jalair walked through the garden and into the house. In his room he undressed slowly, then put out the oil lamp and went to bed.

From the kitchen garden with its pattering fountain, the moon slanted through the open window into Jalair's room. Only that morning he had followed the kestrel's flight through the same window. Now there would be no hawks, and Jalair had needlessly saved them from the rude hands of the Mongol.

Kurush had never intended to buy him the hawks. He had said that only to keep Jalair from talking about them. Now Jalair would live at the Shah's court where it was considered degrading for courtiers to handle and train their own hawks. Kurush, the stranger, and even the Shah, probably thought it honorable to raise Jalair above his father's station.

He saw the task before him. Somehow he must convince Shah Ala-u-Din, ruler of Khoresm, that he would be happiest training to take his father's position as court hawker. Yet, he knew the Shah would be angered at the mention of the Golden Hawks the Mongols had stolen from him when they slew Darien.

He sighed heavily. It was too bad the Golden Hawks were somewhere in the east, being trained and flown for the pleasure of the barbaric Genghis Khan. Because they were, Jalair was doomed to a life empty of the only thing he cared about.

Suddenly he jumped out of bed.

There was a way to make Shah Ala-u-Din change his mind.

Jalair was going to bring the Golden Hawks back to Khoresm.

3 Flight from Samarkand

Jalair knew the parks well, and now he carefully guided his pony to one of the canals that brought river water to the many ponds. At walking pace, he moved from shadow to shadow until he saw the ripple of moonlight on water. Then he turned toward the great wall surrounding Samarkand and its many parks, and found the archway through which the canal ran. There would be just room enough for a horse and rider.

He stopped Rustum in the deep shadows of mulberry and crabapple trees and waited, listening for the steps of the watchmen.

He thought of Kurush, and the stranger from Urgendj, who were sleeping and unaware of Jalair's flight. Perhaps he should have left a note, for they would be angry when they discovered his absence the next morning. Yet there was no way to explain, and if he mentioned the Golden Hawks they would know he had set out for the land of the Mongols. Then it would only be a matter of hours before the Shah's guards would bring him back.

For the same reason he must not be caught by the city's watchmen who circled the walls, patrolled the streets, and guarded the long bridge that crossed the river. Though their duty was to stop thieves and prowlers, they would not hesitate to question a boy on a pony at this late hour, and then summon Kurush to take him home.

Jalair waited until the watchmen cried the hour. The distant calls told him none was near this part of the wall.

Quickly he urged Rustum into the canal. With hardly a splash, Jalair and his pony slipped under the archway connecting with the river. He shivered with the sudden cold wetness. The bundles of supplies tied back of the saddle were soaked. The pony shook his head above the water and worked his legs furiously.

Jalair leaned over the saddle, for the archway was so low he nearly bumped his head. He could smell the dank stale air, and when he put out his hand to steady himself against the tunnel, it came away slippery with slime.

In the pitch blackness, the tunnel seemed much longer

than it was. But at last Jalair smelled fresh air, and saw through the archway the ripple of moonlight on the river.

Then the current caught them, pulling them away from the shore. Rustum whinnied, but with Jalair's urging, the pony bravely worked his legs against the current's pull.

A shout rang out, a command to stop. Glancing back, Jalair saw two guards atop the wall running toward the archway he had just left. The moon glinted on a raised bow.

Jalair was in the middle of the river now, and Rustum was almost exhausted. He allowed the pony to rest while the current swept them downstream around a bend, away from Samarkand and the range of a bow.

Soon the far shore loomed close, and the pony struggled until they reached the bank. Jalair threw himself off and led Rustum into the shadows. There they rested for a long time, and Jalair wrung out his wet clothes. Fortunately, the food in the leather sacks was still dry.

Jalair was about two miles below the caravan route where it crossed the bridge into Samarkand. He struck off at an angle, away from the river, careful to keep in shadows.

After an hour of cautious travel, Jalair found the wide caravan trail, deeply rutted from heavy carts, and pounded hard by the passing of thousands of camels, oxen, and horses. The moon was almost down now. Soon it would be time to stop for the night, and tomorrow morning he would seek employment in the next caravan going eastward.

The trail took him across two shallow rivers, then it rose into the hills. In the moonlight, Jalair could see deep scuffmarks where carts had recently spilled their loads. As the road leveled out in the hills, Jalair noticed torches moving in the distance.

His first thought was of the brigands that often plagued caravans, but surely they would not camp right on the trail itself. Yet a caravan would have no occasion to stop so close to Samarkand. He approached cautiously, holding Rustum down to a walk.

A horse whinnied as it sensed a stranger, and one of the moving torches stopped as a man called out. "Who goes there?"

Jalair rode up to the torch-bearer and dismounted. "I am a traveler. Are you in trouble?"

Another man dressed in rich robes, his jeweled turban winking in the flames, approached and addressed the torch-bearer. "What is the matter, Abdul?"

"It is a traveler who saw our lights," Abdul answered, holding the torch close to Jalair to examine him.

"If the watchmen let him leave Samarkand, then he is honest," answered the rich-robed man. He moved closer to Jalair. "Why, it is a boy! Do you dare travel alone, lad?"

Jalair told him his name, and added, "I seek work in a caravan going east."

"I am Urbano, the Venetian," the man replied. "I am going as far as Khotan. I will give you food and blankets and three coppers a day if you help care for my stock of goods and the animals carrying them."

"I will work willingly," Jalair said, enormously pleased to have found work so quickly. "But why has the caravan stopped so near to Samarkand?"

Preceded by Abdul's torch, Urbano led Jalair to a nearby campfire, where two other servants crowded around a camel lying on the ground. "Some foolish cattle driver started his herd running down the trail without watching for caravan traffic. Our animals were frightened and bolted. We were forced to stop, round them up, and repack our goods. Many animals were injured, as this camel of mine that suffered a kick in the side. With care, it may be able to walk when we start out tomorrow morning."

The Venetian merchant turned to the torch-bearer. "Abdul, this lad will go with us to Khotan. Put him to work."

"Who is this boy?" called out a voice in the darkness.

Jalair peered into the night, but the moon was already behind the trees and he could only make out a shadowed figure on a horse beyond range of the campfire.

"He was not with us when we left Samarkand," the rider continued. He spoke in Arabic, the universal language of the caravan trail. Jalair was glad Sayyid Hussayn had made him study hard.

"He is called Jalair," Urbano answered, also in Arabic. "He joined us this moment, and I have employed him."

"You must take him to Kaban, merchant," the rider answered, his voice ringing with authority. "The leader must approve of everyone in the caravan. Go at once."

The rider turned his horse away. For an instant, firelight gleamed on weapons, and Jalair knew then the man was one of the guards a caravan posts during the night.

"They might wait until morning," Urbano grumbled. "Little did I think you would cause me trouble. Abdul, light our way to Kaban."

Abdul took up the torch and went ahead of Jalair and the merchant. The flames gave feeble light, and Jalair had to watch the ground carefully to keep from stumbling in the age-worn cart tracks. At last they stopped, and before them a curtain was lifted aside, revealing a rectangle of yellow light from the fire within.

Abdul spoke rapidly to Urbano, then stepped aside as the merchant entered the doorway with Jalair at his heels.

"Abdul says Kaban is making the rounds of the camp, and we must wait for him," Urbano said irritably. "Bah! How dare Kaban keep Urbano of Merv, late of Venice, waiting?"

But Jalair hardly heard him, for he was gazing around in astonishment. This was no sort of tent he had ever seen.

Thin wands of wood had been cleverly woven together to form this circular tent. The walls sloped overhead, forming a dome, in the center of which was a hole to allow firesmoke to escape. The wooden framework was covered tightly with a thick material Jalair knew was called felt.

"What kind of tent is this?" he asked curiously.

"They call it a *yurt*," Urbano answered, his temper shortened by the wait for Kaban.

The *yurt* was very large. Part of it was curtained off to form a small separate room, which Jalair guessed was the sleeping compartment. The sloping walls of the *yurt* bore strange-looking bows and quivers of arrows, two swords in decorated scabbards, and a round shield studded with nails.

Abdul called through the curtained doorway, "Kaban comes."

Instantly, Urbano's impatience vanished. He stood humbly, facing the doorway, and Jalair hurried to join him.

The curtain was pushed aside and a man stooped to enter the low doorway.

Before Jalair could even see what this Kaban looked like, Urbano bowed very low, his elbow warning Jalair to do likewise. When Urbano finished his deep bow and nudged Jalair to turn around, Kaban had seated himself in a low chair opposite the doorway.

Jalair's heart squeezed with fear.

Kaban was the Mongol he had seen in Eli's shop.

Urbano was speaking to the caravan leader, but Jalair hardly heard him. What would happen when Kaban recognized him?

Urbano finished speaking and bowed respectfully.

Then the terrible Mongol was looking directly at Jalair with cold, haughty eyes. He studied Jalair for a long time, and the boy wondered if the Mongol could hear his thumping heart. At last Kaban spoke, in faltering Turki. "You speak—Arab tongue?"

"Yes," Jalair answered in that language. "I do."

"Then we shall speak it," Kaban said in fluent Arabic. "I have not yet mastered the Turkic language. When did you leave Samarkand?"

"Tonight," Jalair answered shakily.

"And of course, Shah Ala-u-Din's guards allowed you to pass." A flicker of amusement played across Kaban's face, then vanished. "What have you run away from? Have you stolen?"

Jalair swallowed hard, wishing his throat hadn't turned dry. "I have not stolen anything." Then with sudden inspiration, he added, "My parents are dead."

Kaban's eyes traveled down Jalair's clothes. His tunic was ripped and dirty, his sandals caked with mud. Indeed, he looked like an orphan.

Kaban nodded, apparently satisfied. "Urbano says he will employ you as far as Khotan. What will you do there?"

"I will find work in another caravan going east." The reply slipped out before Jalair realized it.

"What is there in the east that interests you?" Kaban asked sharply.

"The—the lands of Genghis Khan," Jalair faltered.

Kaban waited in icy silence.

"I have heard how Genghis Khan conquered Cathay," Jalair added, trying to think of a reason Kaban would accept. "I wish to visit the court of this mighty ruler," he said. But the words were bitter as he remembered the cowardly attack on his father, Darien.

"I see," Kaban answered coldly. "You may travel with this caravan as long as you do not lie, steal, cheat, or harm others and their belongings. You must obey every order that I, or any other Mongol, might give. Now go."

Urbano's elbow reminded Jalair to bow. Just as he was about to follow the merchant through the low doorway, Jalair saw that the curtain forming the sleeping room was drawn aside. A boy Jalair's own age looked out curiously. He had Kaban's black eyes and hair, and when he saw Jalair looking at him, he broke into a friendly grin.

Urbano spoke only once as Abdul lighted their way back to the merchant's tents. "Jalair, you are to sleep with the servants. Abdul will give you blankets."

Tired after his escape from Samarkand, and relieved Kaban had apparently not yet recognized him, Jalair quickly went to sleep.

Dawn was just struggling over the hills when crashing cymbals awakened the camp to the day's work. Sleepily, Jalair rolled out of his blankets and fumbled for his sandals.

By the pale light coming through the tent's entrance, he saw Urbano's three servants spring to life, rolling up their blankets and starting the breakfast fire.

"Hurry, boy!" Abdul called. "There is work to be done, and it is better done on a full stomach."

Jalair joined them at the fire and was handed a bowl of boiled barley, such as only poor people in Khoresm ever ate. Plainly, Urbano did not become rich by spoiling his servants. Jalair wrinkled his nose at the sticky mass. He ate instead all the cold mutton and dried fruit he had brought along.

"He spurns our food," sneered Abdul, looking enviously at Jalair.

"He will not for long," another servant promised grimly.

Too late, Jalair realized he should have shared his food. But now his food sacks were empty.

The servants cleaned their barley bowls, then kicked out the fire.

"Roll up your blankets and put the tent in order," Abdul ordered Jalair. "Then come outside to load the camels."

Jalair raked dirt over the last embers, then hurried to clean the tent. From the excited babble outside, he knew there was little time to lose. He had just finished packing everyone's belongings in separate bundles when Abdul put his head inside and shouted for him to load the camels.

"I know nothing of animals," Jalair confessed as he followed Abdul to the picket line and saw the great shaggy beasts already tossing their ugly heads in ill-humor.

"Get to work, you lazy boy!" Abdul ordered. "Urbano has told me to see you earn your keep." He pointed to two dozen great earthen jars nearby. "Load four jars of walnut oil on each camel, and take care you do not break them." Then turning on his heel with a swish of his robes, Abdul left Jalair to puzzle out his task alone.

Jalair had, of course, seen many camels in Samarkand with their great loads. He knew the temperamental beasts needed skilled handling, but he knew too that neither Urbano nor Kaban would wait for him to learn his new trade.

Luckily, Abdul had already put the pack frames on the six camels Urbano owned. Jalair found the pile of nets, and managed to get one of the slings around the first jar. Then by pulling and rolling the jar, he worked it to the side of a kneeling camel. The beast, sensing the time for work had come, began thrashing its head, squealing, and spitting. Only the picket rope kept him from getting to his feet. Jalair managed to hoist the jar to the pack frame's rack, but just as he was tying it, the camel stretched his neck and bit Jalair's shoulder. Jalair slapped the head away, and finally got the jar fastened.

Without taking time to rest, he loaded the camel with three more jars, then began on the next in line.

Around him the air was filled with shouts and commands, the squeal of camels, lowing of oxen, snorts of horses, and the pounding of hoofs as the Mongol overseers urged everyone to hurry.

He had only finished loading the second camel when Urbano came over, shouting with impatience, "Hurry, hurry. Kaban will leave us behind! What have you been doing all morning?"

Morning! The sun was just beginning to come over the hills. Jalair glanced around the camp, shocked to see that the multitude of tents and Mongol *yurts* had vanished and the caravan train was already forming.

"Abdul has already loaded the ox-carts," Urbano fumed.

"Spices and cotton bales are easier loaded than oil jars," Jalair said angrily.

"Insolent boy!" Urbano raged. He lifted his hand to cuff Jalair's ear, but the boy sidestepped the blow. Urbano shouted for Abdul, and the three servants came running.

Quickly they shoved Jalair aside and began loading rapidly. "Hitch the oxen," Urbano commanded Jalair.

Jalair ran over to them and began tugging on the halters. There were two of the lumbering brutes for each cart, and Jalair managed somehow to get their harness twisted. He had only straightened it out, not without having one ox step on his foot, when the Mongol riders galloped through the camp shouting in Arabic, "In line, in line!"

Urbano's camels were already in the column, and Jalair led the oxen over. Then he ran to saddle Rustum and tie on his few belongings. Luckily, the servant who had charge of feeding and watering Urbano's animals had already cared for the pony.

The shouting of men and grunts of animals grew as reluctant beasts were pulled into caravan formation. Jalair had just trotted to his place behind Urbano's servants when a long blast was sounded from a horn.

Instantly, all was quiet, and the animals perked up in readiness. Kaban was at the head of the column, his white crest tossing proudly in the morning breeze, and Jalair saw his arm move in signal.

A tall shaft was raised, a carved white eagle at its tip, and nine unfamiliar white tails hung from crossbars beneath.

At once the caravan began to move, each person allowing the cart or horseman in front of him to move ahead before starting. The caravan stretched itself like a snake in the sun and began winding up through the hills.

"Abdul, what does the white eagle mean?" Jalair asked as he jogged along on his pony.

"It is the standard of Genghis Khan," the servant answered gruffly. "Do you not know this is a Mongol caravan? The leader, the guards, every Mongol must be treated with great respect. Even the boy."

Jalair glanced around, and saw the boy he had seen in

Kaban's *yurt* leisurely galloping on his horse. He held a long pole in his hand, a rope noose on its far end. From time to time, the boy would swing low in his saddle and snare in the loop something from the ground—a plant, a rock, or things discarded by past caravans.

"Is that Kaban's son?" Jalair asked. It was easy to see the boy did no work, but passed his time in play.

"Yes. His name is Dhuvik, and, like all Mongols, he must be treated with greater honor than even Khoresmians," Abdul answered bitterly.

When Jalair next glanced at Kaban's boy, he found Dhuvik riding in step with him far to one side. And the young Mongol was gazing with deep interest at Jalair.

"Abdul, I am going to check the oxen's harness." Before the servant could answer, Jalair quickly swung out of line and rode to the oxen ahead, keeping the caravan between him and Kaban's son.

When he returned from this unnecessary job, Dhuvik had galloped out of sight.

Jalair sat straight in his saddle. He had nothing to fear, he reminded himself. There had been no Mongol boy in the market place when he had kept Kaban from buying his goshawks.

Yet, as Jalair knew from his own experience, a boy usually went unnoticed in a crowd.

Throughout the long morning, the caravan climbed through the hills, and by noon it was beginning to inch its way toward the mountain passes.

Then the standard with the nine tails and the white eagle dipped sharply. The caravan slowly came to a halt and the riders began turning out.

Cooking fires were lighted, and Jalair tried to remember the dozen orders Urbano and his servants shouted to him. He set all the animals to grazing, gathered wood for the fire, set out the food supplies, put up the blanket sun shelter demanded by Urbano, and finally was given a bowl of barley. Hunger made Jalair force the hateful food down.

"See how quickly he learns to like our food," Abdul laughed.

The servants shared a few dates among themselves, but

they were gone when Jalair finished his unappetizing meal. "Abdul," he sighed, "how long will it take to reach Khotan?"

Abdul shrugged. "Two weeks, or longer, depending on the weather. Do not forget to clean up our dishes."

Jalair cleaned and put away all the dishes and utensils while the servants took their ease. When he came back from packing them away, he found Dhuvik sitting on horseback, looking at him with great interest. Jalair turned his back to the Mongol boy, but shifted uncomfortably as he felt Dhuvik's eyes still upon him.

Was Dhuvik mocking him? Was he trying to tell Jalair that he recognized him from the market place but had not yet told his father?

Kaban had to be reckoned with also. These Mongols were said to store away all insults and pretend indifference. Then they would suddenly swoop down with all their terrible vengeance.

And there was the curious horseman—the Mongol at the gates of the house of Kurush. Jalair had not yet seen him in the caravan, but the Mongol guards were plentiful and did not care to be stared at by a mere Khoresmian. The horseman could easily remember the well-dressed boy in the courtyard of a fine house. Did the horseman know the house was that of a minor Khoresmian official?

"Abdul," Jalair asked suddenly, interrupting the talk of the servants, "does this caravan contain all the Mongols who come to Khoresm?"

Abdul grunted. "No, praise Allah! We are in one of two caravans. The other goes to the Persian district of our empire. Between the two are sent a great many messengers wearing their copper tiger tablets, for these barbarians so fear Shah Ala-u-Din that they must at all times know where every Mongol is."

So there was a good chance the horseman at the gates would not see him, Jalair thought with relief. The tiger tablet on his chest meant he was a messenger. Yet there was Dhuvik watching his every move, and there was still Kaban who might come to remember Jalair.

"What is our first stop?" Jalair asked after a moment of brooding silence.

"Have you no manners?" Abdul growled, his talk with the others again interrupted. "We reach Khojend in three more days."

"So soon?" Jalair cried in surprise. From the talk in Samarkand's market place, he knew the journey took longer.

"Aye, these Mongols push us until we fall from fatigue," one of the other servants added gloomily.

"They hasten to leave the Shah's authority," Abdul sneered. "Cowards!"

Khojend, in three more days! But perhaps even that would not be soon enough.

Mounted Mongols began rounding up the caravan train, and Jalair ran to his work.

Jalair knew little of the caravan's progress the next three days. His world was made up of balky oxen, heavy jars of walnut oil, mean-tempered camels, ropes that refused to be tied, harness that tangled, fuel gathering, running to the confusing commands of Urbano and his servants, and always and forever the detestable boiled barley that was his only food. And when he chanced to glance up, it was to meet Dhuvik's curious eyes.

He ached with weariness and wanted only to be able, for once, to get a full night's sleep.

And then, suddenly, as joyful as a cool mountain breeze, the caravan reached the Jaxartes River, and, following it, soon came to Khojend.

Cheerfully, Jalair ran to his tasks after the caravan had lumbered into Khojend's market place one afternoon. Urbano bargained for a stall, and Jalair helped unload oil jars, spices and cotton into it. Then the camels and oxen were herded to the public stables, and finally Jalair was assigned a sleeping place in the caravansary, a shelter for traveling merchants.

Happily he sank into the straw and slept deeply.

In the morning, Abdul's foot prodded him awake. "You are to mind the stall this morning, and see you get the prices Urbano has set."

"Where is Urbano?" Jalair asked, cheerful because of his plans.

"Arguing with Kaban in the market place."

Kaban, Jalair found when he went to Urbano's stall, had apparently won the argument, for the Venetian was bowing deeply and calling the Mongol, "Excellent Kaban, wisest of leaders." Urbano's great respect dissolved when Kaban strode away. "Bah!" growled the merchant. "He has ordered me to exchange my stall with someone else."

"Why?" Jalair was curious.

"He says the oil jars that spread out into the street hinder the traffic," Urbano grumbled. "Here, now. Get to work at once moving my goods."

"Urbano," Jalair said firmly. "I wish to be discharged from your service."

"What, what!" cried the merchant, tugging in fury at his beard. "Obey my orders at once!"

"Give me the money I have earned," Jalair said, his resolve cracking a little under Urbano's fury. "I wish to stay in Khojend."

The merchant drew himself up and towered over Jalair. "You agreed to work as far as Khotan," Urbano reminded him. "Where can I find one to replace you?"

"Khojend is a large city," Jalair said. "It would be easy to find another boy. Give me my pay, Urbano. Please."

The gleam of anger left Urbano's eyes. "Of course, Jalair," he said smoothly. "You may go. But first, no one can leave the caravan unless Kaban gives his permission."

Jalair swallowed hard. He hoped to slip away unnoticed by the Mongol. "Then I shall see Kaban."

"One moment." The merchant put his hand on Jalair's shoulder and lowered his voice. "You do not know how ruthless and cruel these Mongols are, Jalair. To ask to leave one of their caravans is a great insult to them. I have heard many times that permission is never granted. Instead, out in the lonely mountains, the person who has committed this insult is thrown over a cliff. It is 'accidental,' naturally."

Yes, Jalair thought in despair, the Mongols would do something like that. They would even seek revenge on a small boy who had escaped one of their murderous assaults years ago.

"Then, give me my pay, so I may buy meat," Jalair said. "I am tired of barley." Without the money he could not escape the caravan.

"No, Jalair," Urbano said in a fatherly tone. "I know you mean to escape, but the Mongols search a city when someone is missing from the caravan train. This too, means death, and I can not let you do this to yourself."

"They would never find me," Jalair insisted.

"I cannot waste time arguing with you," Urbano snapped, impatient with the long talk. "Move my goods to my new stall."

Disheartened, Jalair began struggling again with the heavy earthen jars.

4 A Bow Is Drawn

Kabân's caravan stayed two days in Khojend to complete its business. Then one morning the long blast of a horn sounded, the standard of Genghis Khan was lifted, and the caravan train moved out. Kaban followed the Jaxartes River, setting a fast pace. Two and a half days later the train entered Kokand, a bustling trade city on a great plain that sloped up to meet the Tien Shan—mountains the caravan would soon cross.

Urbano kept Jalair busier than ever in Kokand, and the boy was glad when Kaban's horn signaled their departure from the city. By now, Urbano had sold his walnut oil, spices, and cotton, but Jalair still had to struggle with the great earthenware jars, filled now with pomegranate juice. The Venetian's ox-carts were packed with salt, crabapples, and polished stone ornaments.

Fergana was in the foothills of the Tien Shan, the last city the caravan would see until it had crossed that immense and rugged mountain range. The city was cool, almost cold, but Jalair was kept too busy to notice the chill air. Urbano and the three servants worked him hard, and it was only during the few minutes before he wearily dropped off to sleep each night that Jalair gave a thought to Dhuvik's studying eyes, or to Kaban who might yet recognize him as the boy in Samarkand's market place.

The caravan moved up into cold layers of air as it wound through the passes beyond Fergana. Above him, Jalair could see the mountain glaciers and feel their cold breath through his thin clothes.

The caravan had traveled only a few hours when, to Jalair's surprise, Kaban called a halt.

"What is the matter, Abdul?" Jalair asked, shivering from the cold. "Why have we stopped?"

"We must wait for the yaks," Abdul answered surlily.

"The what?"

"Do not waste time asking questions," the servant ordered as he dismounted. "Get Urbano's animals off the trail at once."

The caravan workers were already pulling their beasts

into the broad fields beside the ancient road. While Urbano and his servants rested, Jalair set to work. The cold made his fingers numb, and he could hardly grasp the halters of the oxen. Two of the camels had promptly knelt down when the caravan halted, and Jalair had to kick them before the stubborn beasts grudgingly rose. At last he was able to rest, yet the cold made it impossible for him to sit still.

"The yaks are coming!" someone shouted.

Jalair looked up, and gasped with astonishment.

Coming down the path from the upper slopes of the mountains was a herd of the oddest animals Jalair had ever seen. They looked something like ordinary oxen, yet they were covered with thick coats of long dark shaggy hair. Each yak was armed with a pair of long curving horns. Their stringy tails ending in a tuft of hair looked ridiculous on the slow-moving animals. Each yak wore an empty pack frame.

"They do not look as if they are good for anything," Jalair said, his teeth chattering.

"Careful how you speak," Abdul warned sharply. He pointed to the standard of Genghis Khan which was stuck in the earth to one side of the trail. "See those nine tails? They are from yaks, for the Mongols prize these silly-looking beasts highly."

At least, Jalair reflected, the absurd animals had warm coats of hair. "Are we going to start soon after they pass?" The movement in the saddle might warm him a little.

Abdul laughed. "Kaban has ordered everyone to load the yaks."

Mongol outriders herded the yaks together near the caravan. Then Kaban's men trotted around, giving the order to begin transferring goods from horses to yaks. Jalair followed Abdul and the other two servants as they joined in the work.

A Mongol pointed to bags of almonds piled high, and spoke to Jalair in Arabic. "Here, boy. Load these bags."

Jalair went to work, hoisting a heavy bag to his shoulder. He shivered from the chill wind, and almost dropped the bag as he handed it to a man who secured it to the yak's pack frame.

Every caravan member was busy untying packs from the horses the Mongols had used, and loading them onto the unwieldy-looking yaks. Even Abdul staggered under a load of wineskins, and, to Jalair's great surprise, Urbano was puffing with bales of licorice root. A Mongol sat on his horse nearby, which explained Urbano's sudden interest in work.

Jalair stopped to beat warmth back into his arms. "Hurry!" called the man tying the sacks to the pack frame. The boy shouldered another bag of almonds, but he was stiff with cold. Moving awkwardly, he dropped his burden and the sack split open, the almonds spilling on the ground.

Urbano had seen the accident. He dropped his bale of licorice root and hurried over. "Now what have you done?" he hissed in anger and despair. "Tie it up at once, before Kaban comes."

But before Jalair could make his stiff fingers fashion the knot, he heard a horse stop near him. It was Kaban.

Urbano was already bowing and smiling. "A thousand pardons, Kaban! The boy is clumsy. I will have him punished."

"Do not punish him," Kaban ordered in a voice as chill as the mountain air. "An injured worker is of no use to my caravan." He studied Jalair, and added, "Nor is a cold one. Merchant, give the boy a warm cloak."

Urbano went white. "A good cloak, for a boy?"

"At once."

The merchant choked back his anger and bowed humbly. He hurried off to his carts, but Kaban did not move until Urbano returned with a warm cloak which Jalair gratefully put on.

"Let him keep it until he is no longer in your service, merchant," Kaban said, and moved on.

"Heathens and pagans!" Urbano snarled when Kaban was out of hearing. "What a country I am in! I never should have left Venice."

Jalair huddled in the cloak until he felt warmer. "Then why do you travel with the Mongols?"

Urbano shook his head sorrowfully. "My goods get better prices under Genghis Khan's standard, for no one dares cheat anyone under a Mongol's protection. And there is no trouble from town thieves and roving brigands on the way." The merchant started back to his work. "Take care you do not ruin that cloak, Jalair!"

Jalair worked hard with the loading. His muscles ached, and he could not walk without staggering. His only comfort was the sight of Urbano puffing under the weight of bundles.

Then his glance fell upon Dhuvik. The Mongol boy did no work, but amused himself trotting around the area. Several times, Dhuvik dashed his horse up a steep slope, whirled at the top, then galloped down at full speed to bring his mount to a rearing stop.

The loading had just been finished when the order came to form the caravan. Jalair trudged to the six camels, pulled them into line, then brought up the ox-carts. Then, mounting his pony, he trotted to his place behind Urbano's goods. The merchant was next to him, grumbling and complaining at having to work, and worse, wasting a new cloak on a worthless boy.

When the caravan began climbing up the trail into the mountains, Jalair saw that the Mongol pack horses were left behind, and the yaks had joined the train. "Urbano, why did we have to transfer the loads to these yaks?"

The merchant left off grumbling long enough to answer. "Those wares are being sent directly to Karakorum, the city of Genghis Khan. Most of the goods would spoil during the journey through the desert Kaban plans to take, so the yaks will soon leave our caravan and strike out to follow the backbone of the Tien Shan, where it is always cold."

"Could not the horses make that journey?" Jalair wondered.

Urbano's injured pride was soothed by the flattery of Jalair's questions, and he answered readily. "The horses the Mongols left behind are from the Oxus Valley region, and they would perish in the cold of the mountains. The Mongol yaks are used to cold, but would perish in the heat of the valleys. Therefore when Kaban journeys toward Samarkand, he has horses brought up while the yaks stay in the high pastures. And he reverses the procedure when he journeys back to Karakorum."

They rode along for a while until a thought troubled Jalair. "Your horses, Urbano. Would they perish in the mountains we must cross to reach Khotan?"

The Venetian shook his head. "The horses I and my servants ride were purchased from the Kipchaks who breed hardy mounts. I have no fears."

But Jalair did. Samarkand was in the broad valley that formed the Oxus Valley region, and his pony had been bred there. Already Rustum was laboring under the strain of all-day riding. What would happen during the icy challenge ahead?

He reached forward to pat Rustum's neck. His pony had gotten him out of Samarkand. Rustum could do anything.

The gradual ascent the caravan had made from the Oxus Valley region gave way to an abrupt and difficult climb. Gentle sloping pastures in the highlands became steeply angled, their edges faced with raw and cruel rocks. Kaban mercilessly pushed men and beasts up through the passes, the more quickly to cross the peaks of the Tien Shan and descend to the milder climate and kinder pastures on the other side of the jagged divide.

Each day the air was sharper and colder. Each day, as he burrowed into the warmth of his cloak, Jalair lifted his face toward the sparkling peaks and found them nearer. Each day, too, Jalair's pony walked slower and slower.

Finally the caravan halted at the last of the twisted and stunted trees, the last of the scant forage. Already they had traveled these last hours through crusty snow. Ahead loomed the final, and highest, pass.

All that day Jalair's pony had lagged behind the caravan, for Rustum often slipped and stumbled in the snow. At last, Jalair dismounted, and though the snow crust cut his sandal-clad feet, he led his pony to join the caravan where it was making camp.

Urbano's tents were already set up when Jalair finally reached the camping place. "Lazy boy!" Abdul shouted at him. "Others have had to do your work while you lingered on the trail. Urbano has been calling for his meal. Take it to him at once."

It was useless to explain about his pony, for Urbano and his servants did nothing but shout at him. Jalair unsaddled Rustum, then ran to his work.

The following dawn when Jalair left the servants' tent to begin his work, he found the cold wind had stiffened to an icy blast. Quickly he ran to Rustum. The pony was on his side, wheezing painfully.

"Get up, Rustum," he urged his pony. "Only one more day. Then everything will be all right." That night would find them on the other side of the Tien Shan.

Jalair coaxed and urged, and finally succeeded in getting Rustum to his feet.

"Jalair, hitch the oxen!" Abdul bellowed from the entrance of the tent.

Jalair hurried with his work to gain time to help his pony nuzzle from beneath the snow the last nourishment before nightfall. Just as the signal to form the caravan was given, Rustum seemed ready for travel.

The standard of Genghis Khan was raised, the caravan jolted forward. Jalair urged his pony to a faster pace, but Rustum only plodded on clumsily, head hanging, breath steaming. Soon they dropped behind the caravan.

Two hours later, there was a halt while the yaks were turned out of the train to make their own journey along the length of the Tien Shan's backbone. Then Kaban's caravan continued without them, though the two parties would meet weeks later before the border of the Gobi Desert.

Up, up the path climbed. The snow deepened, and again Jalair and Rustum were left floundering behind the caravan. They were in the highest pass now, the worst part of the journey.

Suddenly the pony stumbled, lunged forward, then rolled to his side. Jalair pitched into the snow, but he quickly scrambled up to help his pony. Rustum's sides heaved painfully as he gasped for breath.

Jalair glanced around wildly for help. The caravan wound on far ahead. Suddenly a rider turned out of the train and galloped back. It was Urbano.

The merchant reined his horse close to Jalair. "What! Do you dare try to leave the caravan behind my back?"

"Rustum is sick," Jalair said. "Can you help him?"

"You have caused me enough trouble as it is," Urbano cried angrily. "Come along at once!"

Jalair pulled at the reins, but Rustum could only lie wheezing in the snow. "He cannot."

"Very well, then," Urbano growled. "Stay here, and good riddance to a useless idler! Yet I will have my cloak back."

Urbano leaned from his saddle and pulled on the cloak until Jalair almost choked. "Give me my cloak!" the merchant ordered.

"But I will freeze," Jalair protested, gasping for breath.

Urbano had his way. Jalair unfastened the cloak and at once felt the full icy sting of the mountain air. Urbano twitched his horse around.

"You cannot leave me here!" Jalair shouted after him. Already his limbs were numbing from the cold.

Another horseman had turned out of the caravan, and he met Urbano halfway. They exchanged a few words, then the merchant joined the caravan, while the other rider galloped toward Jalair.

It was Kaban.

The Mongol checked his horse, and stared silently at the sick pony.

Jalair wondered if Kaban, finally recognizing him, had come to mock.

With a smooth motion, Kaban slipped out his bow and nocked a murderous-looking arrow. Silently the Mongol drew back the bowstring, and the arrow plunged into the heart of Jalair's pony.

While Jalair's cry of horror still rang among the silent icy peaks, Kaban's arm circled his waist and lifted him to the saddle in front of him.

Without a backward glance at the dead pony, Kaban galloped to the plodding caravan, Jalair clinging to the pommel. The Mongol eased his horse beside Dhuvik's, and spoke swiftly to his son in what Jalair guessed must be the Mongol tongue.

Dhuvik turned his horse out of line. When he returned, he was leading a Mongol horse wearing Jalair's own saddle

and bridle. It crossed Jalair's mind that Kaban must have sent a servant back to where his pony had fallen. Dhuvik's arms were filled with spare clothing.

The three pulled out of the caravan and stopped.

"This is my son, Dhuvik," Kaban explained in Arabic. "You are to ride with him and be his companion, for he finds the journey lonesome. You will sleep in the *yurt* of my servants."

"But what of Urbano?" Jalair protested. "I am in his employ." Better the ill-treatment of Urbano than the uncertain fate Kaban had planned for him.

"Urbano told me he discharged you," Kaban said. "Does he owe you money?"

"Yes," Jalair answered, shivering in his thin tunic. "He promised three coppers a day, to be paid when we reached Khotan."

"He has been cheating you," Kaban said, then trotted off to the head of the caravan.

Dhuvik nudged him, and pointed to the pile of clothing he had brought. The boy said something, but as he spoke only Mongolian, Jalair could not understand. But the clothes were obviously for him.

Jalair pulled on a thick pair of woolen trousers. He kicked off his worn sandals and put on the fur-lined leather boots. Then came a shirt of soft deerskin, and over this Jalair put on a thick woolen jacket lined with sheepskin. Last of all was a fur-lined cap with flaps coming down over the ears, and heavy mittens. He was now dressed like Dhuvik, and it was wonderful to be truly warm again.

Dhuvik handed him the reins of his new mount. From the horse's rangy lines, Jalair knew it came from the herd of Mongol horses that traveled along as replacements for Kaban's men.

Both boys mounted, and with Dhuvik leading, they galloped up and down the dangerous mountain slopes. Jalair was pleased with his new mount. The horse had spirit and strength, and never seemed to tire, nor to slip in the treacherous snow and ice of the pass.

Now that Jalair knew he was not to be left behind to perish, he realized it was mercy which led Kaban to put Rustum out of his misery.

As the caravan began descending on the other side of the dangerous pass, Dhuvik and Jalair dismounted to watch carts and beasts of burden winding down the trail.

Then Dhuvik began pointing to things, giving their Mongolian names. Jalair carefully repeated the words after him, committing them to memory. He was glad Sayyid Hussayn had drilled him in languages, for now he grasped this new tongue easily.

Dhuvik seemed more cheerful than before when he galloped and played by himself. As he rode beside his new friend, Jalair suddenly thought that Dhuvik's stares might have been a longing to make friends.

The day passed swiftly and happily for Jalair. He liked the cold mountain wind now that it no longer chilled his bones. He gloried in the sight of the precipitous cliffs, and the feel of a good horse under him. Several times he burst into laughter just because he felt good, and Dhuvik laughed with him. All he needed now, Jalair thought, was a hawk on his wrist.

The sudden recollection of his journey's purpose dimmed his joy. Quickly he thrust aside the thoughts of the Golden Hawks and his father's death. Dhuvik, at least, had had no part in the terrible affair.

Late that evening as the *yurts* of the Mongols mushroomed amid the tents of the caravan, Jalair ran to join Kaban's servants. But they laughed and good-naturedly pushed him away when he tried to help.

"Your only work is to ride with my son," said Kaban from behind.

Jalair whirled to find Kaban sitting on his horse. Did the man never walk on the ground as did other people?

Kaban held out a bulging leather sack. Hesitantly, Jalair took it. "It is your pay from Urbano," Kaban said. "Ten coppers a day, the sum all caravan workers earn." He turned his horse away before Jalair recovered from his astonishment.

Jalair ate in the *yurt* of Kaban's servants, and the Mongol fare was rich to his hungry eyes. There was boiled meat, rice, cheese, and even fresh milk. The meal ended with generous portions of dried fruits and nuts. Jalair was pleased that out of the swift talk of the men he ate with he could understand the words Dhuvik had taught him that day.

After the meal, one of the Mongols gave Jalair thick wool blankets, and pointed out where he was to sleep. The circular *yurt* gave everyone a chance to sleep near the fire at its center.

The next morning, as the caravan plodded down the steep mountain trail, Dhuvik began teaching Jalair how to use his bow and arrows. Jalair also practiced with the Mongol boy's lasso, and he suddenly realized what skill it took to snare something from the ground at full gallop as Dhuvik did.

The days on the caravan trail passed swiftly as Jalair and Dhuvik tried their horses' skill on steep slopes and cliff edges. The two often went hunting, and it was a proud day when Jalair brought down his first hare. Jalair's command of the Mongol tongue increased until he could talk long and fluently with Dhuvik.

One day as they balanced their mounts on a rocky ledge, Dhuvik pointed to a distant cliff. "Look, Jalair. A sheep!" Quickly he drew his bow and nocked an arrow while Jalair waited breathlessly. Surely the sheep was too far away to hit. Jalair could barely see the white hairy coat and the long curving horns.

Then came the ping of the released bowstring, and the arrow winked in the sun. Dhuvik's aim was true, and, in spite of the incredible distance, the arrow hit its mark. Jalair galloped with his friend to the prize.

"Some day you will be able to do that, Jalair." Dhuvik laughed at Jalair's astonishment. "Now help me skin the sheep before my father wonders if we are lost."

Together they skinned the animal and prepared it for packing on their horses. Cleverly working a thick-bladed knife, Dhuvik detached the curved horns and handed them to Jalair. "These make fine drinking vessels," he said.

"But these are your horns," Jalair protested. "You earned them."

"Then take them as a gift," Dhuvik replied cheerfully.

That night after the evening meal, Jalair sought out a merchant of knives and traded one of the big sheep horns for a sharp dagger. Then he began working on the remaining horn. Kaban, who seemed not to recognize Jalair after all, had been kind. And Dhuvik was a wonderful friend. To show his thanks, Jalair planned a present for Kaban's son.

The days passed quickly as the caravan descended from the peaks and crags of the Tien Shan. Jalair had a wonderful time following Dhuvik, who was quick to find adventure among the cliffs, and later the forests, of the mountains. In idle moments, Jalair worked on the horn he was carving.

"What is it you hide when I approach?" Dhuvik asked one day.

"You will soon find out," Jalair answered, enjoying his air of mystery.

Now that Jalair no longer spent every waking hour working hard in the caravan, he could lift his head more often, and soon he was noticing many fine hawks. Every day there was at least one of the hunters soaring and waiting.

One day Dhuvik watched with Jalair as a peregrine circled overhead, then suddenly plunged downward, wings against its body, curved talons ready for the final blow.

"A good stoop!" Dhuvik cried approvingly.

"Do you like hawks, too?" Jalair asked quickly. Perhaps they could catch one on the trail!

Dhuvik laughed. "Hawking is indeed a fine sport, but I would rather gallop after hares or practice swordplay."

The caravan finally left the mountain barrier behind it and entered Kashgar. This rich trade city nestled in the foothills of the Tien Shan, right on the edge of the dread Takla Makan desert. Like others in the caravan, Jalair laid aside his thick jacket, mittens, and fur cap. He could not work on the horn the two days in Kashgar, for Dhuvik was constantly at his side as they explored the city.

After Kashgar, the caravan followed the ancient road on the edge of the desert. They spent a day at Yarkand, where two discontented workers left the caravan. Kaban seemed not to notice their absence, and Jalair knew then that Urbano had lied to keep him working at unfair wages. The train started for Khotan, the last Khoresmian city Kaban would visit.

It was shortly after leaving Yarkand that Jalair finished the drinking horn he was carving for Dhuvik. The decoration was the only design he knew, the plunging hawk following a jagged lightning bolt earthward. It seemed a fitting picture, for it conjured up the happy days spent with Dhuvik as they galloped together, hunted with bow and arrow, or rode to a mountain ridge to look in silence at the view below.

It was as they rested from a gallop and were watching the caravan plod past on the flat desert's edge that Jalair brought out the horn, laboriously carved and carefully polished. "This is the mystery I have been keeping," he said.

"What a fine drinking horn!" Dhuvik exclaimed. "Did you do this yourself?"

"It is for you," Jalair said, thrusting it into his hands.

"But I cannot take it," Dhuvik protested. "You have been working very long and hard on it."

Jalair insisted, and Dhuvik's broad grin was thanks enough for him.

"That is a fine hawk you carved," Dhuvik said, examining the design closely. "It looks as if it were alive." He picked up his reins. "Let's show it to my father."

Together they galloped to the head of the line, where Kaban rode beside the man who bore Genghis Khan's standard.

"It is a fine piece of work," Kaban said, turning the horn over in his hands. "And Jalair really did this all by himself?"

"Yes, I did," Jalair said proudly. Though Kaban smiled seldom, Jalair had lost his fear of Dhuvik's father.

It was when the caravan was only a day's journey from Khotan that Kaban trotted back to where Jalair and Dhuvik rode side by side in the train. "Dhuvik, will you count the number and kind of animals in the caravan?" Kaban asked. "My records are confused, and I must declare the figure to the guards at Khotan."

Dhuvik turned out of the line, and Kaban rode silently beside Jalair.

"You seem to have some interest in hawking," Kaban said after a long silence.

"The birds are interesting to watch," Jalair answered cautiously, wondering what Kaban was leading up to.

"You must have studied hawks well," Kaban said. "The carving on Dhuvik's drinking horn was expertly done. Or again, you might have copied the design from another you saw."

"I did not copy the design," Jalair said. "It is one of my own making."

"Can you carve pictures of other animals?" Kaban asked.

"No, only the hawk."

"You carved it well, and it is a credit to your skill," Kaban went on. "Such a carver as you need not be ashamed of having borrowed a design. Where have you seen this picture before, Jalair?"

Jalair's heart started beating faster. What did the design mean to Kaban? "I know only that I have never seen this picture before," Jalair answered truthfully.

"Yet you carve nothing else," Kaban pointed out.

"I find hawks more interesting to carve than other things," Jalair replied, holding the reins tighter in his fear.

"In truth, hawks are the finest creatures alive," said Kaban. "At one time I had many of them. Yet my duties with the caravans leave so little time for hawking that I gave my birds to friends. Still I find time enough to examine the hawk shops of almost every city I visit."

Jalair remembered the incident in Samarkand's market place. He held his breath, waiting for Kaban to mention it.

But the Mongol continued to talk of hawking, asking Jalair many technical questions. He seemed satisfied with Jalair's answers. "My interest now lies in horses and camels, however," Kaban concluded.

Abruptly the Mongol left Jalair's side and leisurely cantered to the head of the column.

Jalair did not know what meaning Kaban read into the design of hawk and thunderbolt. The Mongol's deep interest was upsetting enough in itself.

Khotan was but a day away.

It was there Jalair would leave the caravan.

5 A Horn of Trouble

At dawn the next day, the caravan sighted the mud walls of Khotan, baked to a chalky white by the hot sun. By midmorning they reached the city gates, and Kaban declared the quantity and kind of goods to the governor's guards.

Jalair noticed that Urbano eagerly selected the best items of his stock and presented them as gifts to the guards. Other merchants were also opening packs, and when a guard glanced at the goods a merchant was quick to offer him what he would take.

"Why do they give gifts to the guards?" Jalair asked Dhuvik. "Khotan is no greater than other Khoresmian cities."

"Why, Jalair! This gift-giving, as you call it, has gone on at the gates of every city the caravan has entered."

"I never noticed it before," Jalair said. "But it seems strange that besides paying duty on their goods, the merchants would give them away."

Dhuvik laughed. "Gifts indeed! It is nothing but thievery. Khoresmian city governors are a greedy lot, and they instruct their guards to take the most valuable goods from passing caravans. But you will not see my father give in to their threats."

Before Jalair could answer, he noticed Kaban had ordered two horses to be loaded with goods. A guard spoke a few words to Kaban, and Jalair saw the Mongol shake his head as he answered, "I will take them to the Shah's governor myself."

"Why does Kaban trouble himself?" Jalair asked Dhuvik. "If he desires to give gifts to the governor, he can present them to the guards."

"We want to be friends with Khoresm, and give gifts to show our good intentions," Dhuvik said. "But we allow no governor to steal from us what he would. This is why my father goes to the governor's palace in every Khoresmian city, to show we are not frightened by the guards' threats."

"No Khoresmian governor would steal," Jalair said stiffly. "If merchants wish to give gifts, that is their own affair."

Again Dhuvik laughed. "Jalair, you know so little of your own country! These governors, and even the Shah himself, are all greedy for riches."

Jalair's cheeks flamed with anger, but it would not do to call attention to himself when he was about to slip away from Kaban. A Mongol, he remembered, never forgot an insult.

Dhuvik dismissed their argument. "Come on, Jalair. A merchant of gems told me one could pick up jade in Khotan's river. Let us see if we can find some."

Leaving their mounts with the Mongol in charge of horses, they hurried through the city's winding streets. Jalair had become so accustomed to Khoresm's trade cities that he no longer was anxious to explore every stall and shop he saw. On the bank of the Khotan River, where it flowed through the city, the boys took off their boots, rolled up their trousers, and waded into the water.

"What does rough jade look like?" Jalair asked, pretending interest in the search.

Dhuvik pushed up his sleeve and plunged his arm into the water. "Here is a small piece of poor quality." He tried to explain what to look for, but words failed him. Scouting around, he brought up another, better piece. "This second piece is worth keeping. Now can you see the difference?"

Jalair shook his head. "They look alike to me."

Dhuvik laughed and cast away the worthless chip. "Then keep everything you find and let me pick out the good jade."

"You look downstream, and I will go upstream," Jalair suggested. "That way, we can cover more ground."

Dhuvik agreed and started off.

Jalair slowly waded upstream, head bent as if looking for jade. Occasionally he plunged his arm in the river, picked up a stone, then tossed it away. From time to time, Dhuvik called out reports on his progress, but as the boys worked farther apart, his shouts faded, then ceased.

Glancing downstream, Jalair saw Dhuvik disappear around a bend. Quickly wading to shore, he ran to where he had left his boots. For a moment he stood there, thinking of all the good times he had had with his first friend. But there was Kaban and the unfortunate design Jalair had innocently carved on Dhuvik's horn.

He pulled on his boots and walked rapidly away from the river.

Jalair kept away from the central market place where Kaban's caravan would be conducting its business until ready to leave in the afternoon. Instead, he roamed through the residential district and the few parks Khotan boasted, none half as beautiful as Samarkand's. Once he passed the iron gates of an imposing house and, glancing into the courtyard, he saw a boy playing alone with a ball. The boy looked up, then gazed longingly at Jalair.

Thus had Jalair himself often gazed beyond the gates of the house of Kurush, wishing he had the freedom of the boys who ran in the streets. He passed on quickly. He had his freedom now, and found it filled with danger.

And there was no turning back until he recovered the Golden Hawks.

Jalair passed his time looking at the few shops scattered through the residential section, but he was interested only in the time of the day. At sunset, he would be out of Kaban's reach. In the meantime, it would save awkward questions if Jalair stayed out of sight.

Tomorrow, Jalair thought as he wandered, he would find some work in the city, and then join the next caravan east. From Dhuvik, Jalair had learned of Kaban's frequent absences from Karakorum in attending to matters of trade. It would be easy to avoid the Mongol in Genghis Khan's city. And Jalair would be careful never again to carve the mysterious design.

The sun slanted through the narrow streets. By now, the caravan had left, though Jalair would not go near the market place until sundown to be certain. But he felt freer, and when he discovered a hawk shop, he stopped to examine the birds and talk with the owner.

Jalair was just admiring a black shahin with rust-colored breast, a hawk from the Hind country, when he heard a voice behind him.

"The caravan is ready, Jalair," Kaban said.

Jalair jumped, and his heart pounded so hard he could scarcely get his breath. He turned around and forced himself to look at the Mongol steadily, hiding his fear. "Then I must hurry to say good-by to Dhuvik," he said.

"No need of that," Kaban answered, his eyes boring into Jalair. "You are coming with us to Karakorum."

"But we are in Khotan," Jalair protested, trying to keep his legs from trembling. "This is as far as I would have gone with Urbano."

"Do you not remember what you told me the night you joined the caravan?" Kaban said. "You wished to see the court of Genghis Khan. You will see it the sooner if you travel with me."

Kaban took his arm, gently but firmly, and they walked in the direction of the market place. The caravan was already formed, and Kaban took Jalair to his horse.

"Tonight," the Mongol commanded softly, "you will move your blankets into my *yurt*."

Jalair shook his arm free of the hated hand, and quickly mounted.

Dhuvik trotted up beside Jalair. "I thought you were

lost," he said. "I called many times, but you did not answer. When I went to get my boots, yours were gone."

"I became confused over recognizing jade," Jalair said. "I got my boots, then meant to walk downstream to join you. Somehow I lost my way and wandered through the city. But your father found me."

"It is well he did, or you might have been left behind," Dhuvik said. "I found two good pieces of green jade, and one of yellow. Look what I traded them for." He fumbled in his jacket, then held up a leather belt inlaid with brass.

Jalair tried to appear interested as he admired the belt. Before Dhuvik could notice his dark mood, the signal was given and the caravan paced out of the market place.

Most of the merchants who joined the caravan at Khotan were Cathayans. Some were Kashgai from the tribes living on the south margin of the Takla Makan, the desert through which the route now ran. Most Kashgai were nomadic herders, but some had settled in cities as traders and artisans. The remaining travelers were Uigurs.

As the caravan moved out of Khotan, following the riverbank and casting long blue shadows, Jalair noticed for the first time the rhythmic tinkle of bells fastened to each animal, including his own mount.

"What are the bells for?" he asked.

"So that anyone who becomes lost can easily find his way back to the caravan."

"But surely, the noises of the caravan itself would guide him back," Jalair said. "The carts squeak, the animals snort and bellow. And the men talk and call out."

Dhuvik shook his head. "But these are the same noises the goblins make."

"Goblins!" Jalair all but shouted. "Only ignorant people believe in such things."

Dhuvik grinned. "We only call them that. Our scholars say the noises are made by the wind playing across the hollows in the sand, just as a musician blows across the holes of a flute. These 'goblin' sounds travel a great distance, and often cause echoes which further confuse a lost man."

"But the bells guide him to the real caravan," Jalair added.

It was the same reason hawkers put bells on the legs of their birds. If a hawk became lost, or went to ground, the hawker could easily trace it.

"I don't hear any goblins," Jalair said after a pause.

"Not yet," Dhuvik agreed. "We must be farther out in the desert. But the sounds will frighten you if you have not heard them before."

The sun threw out long red rays as it touched the horizon. "Will we soon camp?" Jalair asked.

Dhuvik shook his head. "We will travel all day and most of the night, for my father is anxious to cross the Takla Makan. It is a very terrible desert, Jalair, and few caravans ever come this way."

"Will he not become lost during the night?" Jalair asked. Though there had been times on the trail that Kaban kept the caravan going after nightfall, it had been easy to follow the well-marked road. But here, there was nothing but trackless wasteland, and the fields of grass surrounding Khotan were beginning to lose themselves in the desert sands.

"We will follow the Khotan River," Dhuvik told him. "It will soon turn north, crossing the worst part of the desert. Then we take another river to the east. It's hard for a Mongol to get lost, for we live on vast prairies and are accustomed to noticing landmarks others cannot see."

The caravan traveled until late that night. At first Jalair thought it would be impossible for him to stay in the saddle that long, but he soon copied Dhuvik's trick of bracing himself upright in order to doze a little as his horse followed the one in front of it.

The camp was quickly set up, as everyone was anxious to eat and then sleep, for they would start before dawn. Jalair remembered that Kaban had ordered him to the Mongol's own *yurt*, and as he walked toward it with Dhuvik, he asked, "Why does your father take such an interest in me?"

Dhuvik was puzzled. "What do you mean, Jalair?"

"Urbano would have left me in the mountains with a dying pony, but Kaban clothed and sheltered me. And when we were in Khotan, he made the caravan wait until he found me. And now I am to sleep in his *yurt*."

"Is such treatment of orphan boys unknown in your country?" Dhuvik asked in surprise. "In our land, no boy or girl is ever left to fend for himself. Everyone is fond of young people and tries to make it easy for them."

When they entered Kaban's *yurt*, they were met with a cheerful fire and plenty of good food. A servant began serving them as they sat near the fire, the heat welcome in the cold desert night.

"Father said he will be late for the meal," Dhuvik said, holding out a horn for the servant to fill with fresh milk. To Jalair's astonishment, the horn was not the one he had carved.

"What, Dhuvik!" he exclaimed. "Have you lost your gift already?"

"Oh, no! My father keeps it with him," Dhuvik laughed. "He said I might lose it on the journey."

Jalair suddenly found it hard to swallow.

Kaban had read some secret meaning in the design Jalair had carved. He had searched for Jalair in Khotan. He had ordered Jalair to sleep in his own *yurt*, which nightly was well guarded.

In leaving Khotan, the caravan had left Shah Ala-u-Din's Khoresm. They were now in Genghis Khan's empire, and Jalair was at Kaban's mercy.

Before dawn, the camp was aroused by the crashing cymbals. In a moment breakfast fires were lighted, trail rations for the day distributed, *yurts* and tents were struck, and the long column formed.

They plodded on steadily through the long and tiresome hours. Yesterday's high-spirited talk among the caravan members today settled down to a few comments about the work at hand, or an exchange of accounts of other caravan trails. Over the pacing train of men and animals came a spirit of calm determination—to cross this terrible desert in haste, yet to conserve the energy of men and beasts.

Already the grassy belts on the banks of the Khotan River thinned and narrowed. The river flowed sluggishly through the sands that stretched out as far as the eye could see, relieved only by patches of dry tamarisk and thorn bush, where grass did not grow.

"Listen!" Jalair cried suddenly as he rode beside Dhuvik. The wailing moan came again. "Someone is in trouble. Do you hear him groaning?"

"Goblins." Dhuvik grinned. "You will hear yet stranger sounds, Jalair."

"But it sounded so real!" He could hardly believe the sound was nothing more than air currents playing in sand hollows.

From time to time during the rest of the day's journey, Jalair heard the groaning. He even heard hoofbeats in the distance, and once in a while the creak of ghost ox-carts. He could not help but jump every time he heard a new sound, and when, toward nightfall, he heard a chorus of singing voices, he looked questioningly at Dhuvik.

"Yes, those are the sounds desert travelers hear," Dhuvik said. "We will also hear them when we cross the Gobi. Now listen to my warning, Jalair. You must never gallop after those sounds, no matter how certain you are that they are real."

Jalair saw that no one else in the caravan paid any attention to these strange noises. And, as the journey continued, he too became accustomed to them.

The caravan covered ground rapidly, for not only did the train double its traveling time by giving up much of its nightly sleep, but there were frequent changes of riders and cargo to the reserve camels and horses that had been brought along. The pace was very tiring to Jalair. His only thought was to stay in the saddle during the long days, and to sleep deeply the few hours permitted. He even ceased worrying about Kaban's plans for him and the carved horn.

Water was always with them, for they followed the river northward. But forage for the animals began thinning alarmingly. Camels could still feed on the scrubby thorn bushes of which they were fond, but the horses suffered between the scarce patches of plants and grass. Kaban drove the caravan at an even faster pace to a grazing area he knew they would reach in several days.

One afternoon as Jalair was dozing in the saddle, his mount suddenly lifted its head and whinnied. The reins were torn from his hands as his horse plunged ahead.

"Jalair, hold him, hold him!" Dhuvik cried, fighting with his own unruly mount.

The entire caravan broke up into a riot of shouts and pounding hoofs. Riders flung themselves out of the saddle to pull down their rearing mounts. Jalair managed to get his horse under control, as did most of the other riders. But the pack horses and the reserve mounts broke away, heading toward a patch of green.

Mongol riders galloped after them, shouting and snapping their whips. Dust boiled up around the stampeding horses. Finally the riders headed off the charge, and succeeded in herding the horses back to the river.

"What are they doing?" Jalair cried indignantly. "Kaban has been looking for forage!"

"This is no forage for horses," Dhuvik replied. "The plants are poisonous. All the horses would have died soon after eating."

"Poison! How do you know?"

"If you hold my horse, I will bring a plant and show you."

Dhuvik dismounted and handed Jalair the reins. When he came back he gave Jalair a small leafy plant.

"But this looks just like other plants the horses have eaten," Jalair said, turning it over in his hands.

Dhuvik tried to explain the difference, but failed. It was like trying to put the qualities of good jade over bad into words. "But it is poison," he insisted. "Usually horses will not touch it, unless they're very hungry."

Luckily, good grass was found the next dawn, for Kaban had driven the caravan on without a single hour of rest to reach the graze he knew was near.

All that day, Kaban allowed the caravan to rest while the horses ate their fill. Dhuvik and Jalair stripped off their clothes and enjoyed a swim in the river.

"When we return to Karakorum," Dhuvik said as they lay on the bank, "I will have a week of idleness before I enter the student officers' school. This is my last free time, for the school means several years of hard work."

"Do you have to enter the army?" Jalair asked.

Dhuvik laughed. "No, but almost all the boys want to join. I plan to be an officer like my father is. Last year I

served as a messenger for the army, a requirement for all boys my age. I saw many battles from hilltops, and now I want nothing more than to take my place among the warriors."

"It would not give me much pleasure to take part in raids on other people," Jalair retorted sharply.

"There is no raiding except against enemies," Dhuvik told him. "The army is for the protection of our lands and caravans. Years ago when the Mongols were separated into many small tribes, they fought with one another continually. Genghis Khan changed that when he united the tribes under his standard. Then neighboring kingdoms tried to conquer us and take away our lands. Genghis Khan defeated them one by one. Cathay too, made a mistake when the Golden Emperor sent his soldiers against tribes friendly to us. They asked for help, and the Khan gathered a great army with which he conquered Cathay. After that, Karakhitai, the kingdom through which we are traveling right now, invaded our lands. Genghis Khan drove them out, then went on to add the kingdom to his empire."

This was a far different story from the one Jalair had heard in Khoresm. Yet Dhuvik seemed to believe it completely. "If what you say is true," Jalair said cautiously, "then the Mongol warriors are the bravest in the world."

Dhuvik nodded. "The name 'Mongol' means 'the Brave People.' Now you understand why I will be proud to help keep order inside the empire, and to protect it from invaders."

After the day of rest, the caravan pushed on with great speed, following the Khotan north until it met the Tarim River. Now it turned east along the Tarim, between the dread Takla Makan on the right hand, and the shadows of the extensive Tien Shan range on the left. Days later, the caravan camped for another day's rest beside a great lake.

"We are almost out of the Takla Makan," Dhuvik told Jalair. "We will leave the river now, for it turns south and finally empties into a lake called the Lop Nor."

They pushed on to Turfan, a sizable trade city with a river of its own. Now once again Kaban's train was on a regular caravan trail, and though they still skirted the Takla Makan, they no longer needed to fear the great desert.

"Whose horses are those?" Jalair asked when Turfan loomed ahead on the caravan road.

On the outskirts of the city was a great corral with many fine mounts. Nearby stood mud buildings, and Jalair could see Mongol guards at their various duties.

"The horses are branded with the name of Genghis Khan," Dhuvik said. "Along the regular caravan trails throughout the empire, Genghis Khan has post stations like this built to aid travelers and furnish fresh horses for his messengers. Do you know, Jalair, that it takes only five days, riding day and night, for a message to reach Genghis Khan from the farthest point of his empire?"

It was hard to believe, yet Jalair knew the Mongols were the sturdiest riders ever known.

When the caravan reached the post station, Kaban halted the column and waited as a Mongol came from one of the buildings and walked up to him. The copper tablet on his chest with its beaten tiger design meant he was a messenger of the Khan. Kaban spoke rapidly to the man, and though Jalair was close by, he could not hear what was said. But he did see what Kaban handed to the Mongol.

"Why must we wait?" a merchant grumbled impatiently.

Dhuvik turned in his saddle. "My father is sending a message of arrival to Genghis Khan. We will start soon."

Jalair watched the Mongol with the tiget tablet run to a saddled horse, slip the picket line, jump on and gallop off in a burst of speed and dust. Genghis Khan would receive the message days before the caravan's arrival. He would also have the carved horn Jalair saw Kaban put into a leather pouch and hand to the messenger.

The caravan pushed on to Qomul on the eastern edge of the Takla Makan. There the route split, as one road led to Cathay, the other to Karakorum. There also was a half-day's wait before the yaks that had been sent along the backbone of the icy Tien Shan joined Kaban's train.

Then Kaban led them through the Altai Mountain passes, some still choked with snow in spite of the summer's advance. They dropped down into the Gobi Desert, much cooler than the Takla Makan, yet almost as desolate. Again Jalair heard the desert goblins beating invisible drums, whispering and laughing, playing lutes, and driving their ghostly caravans over the dunes.

Then the sand gave way to grass, which grew taller and taller as they wound northward. The ground bulged into low hills, dotted with immense herds of horses, yaks, and sheep. Herders often galloped up for the latest news, and most seemed to be boys younger than Jalair. They passed more post stations, but Kaban never stopped at these to send other messages.

Finally, laboring over steep hills and through a difficult pass, the caravan sighted Karakorum before them on the plain below.

"Karakorum!" The word was shouted up and down the train. Mongols reared their horses and laughed at being so near to home. The Cathayans, Kashgai, and Uigurs grinned and talked eagerly of opening their markets and shops.

For Jalair there was no rejoicing.

Somewhere among the *yurts* and buildings below were the Golden Hawks.

And somewhere too, Genghis Khan, with the carved horn, awaited him.

6 The City of Genghis Khan

"Father says you are to come with us to see the Khan," Dhuvik told Jalair, while around them Karakorum's market place bustled with excitement and wonderful confusion. Kaban was busy settling the various merchants in their stalls and shops, assigning caravansary space and stables, and judging disputes among the merchants.

Jalair took little note of Dhuvik's words, for he was still marveling over this unusual Karakorum, the only true city in the Mongol's ancient homeland.

The city of Genghis Khan straddled the broad Orkhon River that wound through an immense valley hemmed by mountains on all sides. Karakorum was built, Jalair had seen as the caravan entered, like a series of rings set within one another.

The outer ring was made up of carts of tremendous size and strength. Dhuvik told Jalair these huge wooden platforms set upon wheels were called *kibitkas*. "When a family wishes to move, or to follow its flocks to winter pastures, the household *yurt* is mounted on the platform. There the family lives, while twenty yaks pull the *kibitka* to new grounds."

The household *yurts* of which Dhuvik spoke formed the second ring. These domed tents of felt were much larger than the trail-*yurts* the Mongols used on the caravan route. Yet Dhuvik assured him that even these gigantic *yurts* could be taken down or put up within an hour. Most of the household *yurts* were painted with battle scenes, horse races, wrestlers, and other pictures.

The center of the large city was formed of mud buildings —granaries, stables, shops, caravansaries, and storehouses. To reach the market place, the caravan crossed the Orkhon on a broad stone bridge, built by Cathayan engineers.

At last Kaban finished his work in the market place, and taking Genghis Khan's yak-tailed, white eagle standard, he mounted and led the way to the court.

The three trotted through the winding pathways between mud buildings, and came to a great open area circled by huge painted *yurts*. In the center of this space was a *yurt* of pure white felt, surely the largest structure in the entire city!

Before it stood ranks of armed guards, their lacquered leather breastplates and polished weapons gleaming. Nearby was struck into the earth a great shaft, tipped with the nine white yak tails and carved white eagle of Genghis Khan.

Jalair could not take his eyes from the huge white *yurt*. Untouched by any decoration, it looked like a cloud.

"That is the *yurt* of Genghis Khan," Dhuvik told him.

They dismounted near the armed guards at the entrance of the Khan's *yurt*. Dhuvik and Kaban took off their swords, bows and quivers and handed them to the guards.

"No one may enter the Khan's presence while bearing weapons," Dhuvik explained.

Jalair took off his sheathed knife and handed it to a guard.

In spite of the size of the *yurt*, the entrance was the usual low doorway covered by a felt curtain. Kaban stooped to enter, followed by the boys. Jalair blinked in the sudden gloom. Kaban ordered in a low voice, "Stay here until called," then went forward with a guard who announced him to the Khan.

The far end of the *yurt* toward which Kaban walked was ablaze with light spilling from two brass bowls burning scented woods, and from dozens of lamps and torches fastened to the curving *yurt* walls. The smoke twined upward and found its way through the opening in the center of the domed roof.

In the light of the brilliant flames sat a man on a carved and lacquered throne. Kaban bowed low, handed over the standard that had guided the caravan across mountains and through deserts, and began giving his report of the journey.

Jalair's view of Genghis Khan was hidden by the tall figure of Kaban, and his attention shifted to armed guards standing on both sides of the Khan's throne. Another man sat on a cushion nearby, a writing board on his knees, a quill in his hand. He wore the robes of a Cathayan, and Jalair guessed he must be Genghis Khan's scribe.

Beyond the brilliant circle of light, Jalair made out other figures, some standing, some sitting. Many wore bright cloaks and brilliantly lacquered armor.

"Who are those men?" Jalair whispered to Dhuvik.

"They are Masters of the Court, each with special duties. Their cloaks show their titles," Dhuvik whispered back. "There is the Master of Hunting, the Master of Herds, the Master of Student Officers, and many others."

"Do they spend all their time in this *yurt?*"

"No, but they come frequently to tell the Khan of their work, or merely to pass the time."

Kaban turned around and beckoned to the boys. Jalair followed Dhuvik down the long white horseskin carpet that led to the throne, but he could not resist stealing glances at the many strange weapons that hung on the sloping felt walls.

Dhuvik bowed low before the Khan, and Jalair was quick to follow his example.

The Khan greeted Dhuvik in friendly fashion. "Did you enjoy your trip to the west?" he asked.

"Very much, my Khan," Dhuvik answered, entirely at ease. He went on to describe the many things that fascinated him in the western country. While he spoke, Jalair studied the conqueror.

Dhuvik had told him the Khan was over six feet tall, but

Jalair had never expected to see such broad shoulders, nor such large strong hands. Long red hair and a beard to match went well with the intelligent gray eyes. Dressed quite like the ordinary Mongols, the Khan wore red lacquered breastplates, woolen trousers tucked into black boots, and a belt of linked gold plates.

Behind the Khan, hung on a peg in the *yurt's* framework, was a plain cloak of sable, and a battle helmet crested with a white yak tail.

Surely, thought Jalair, no other conqueror had lived and dressed as simply as this.

"And now for the other lad," the Khan said in his deep voice.

With the Khan's steady gray eyes upon him, Jalair wondered if he should bow again. Seeking a cue, he glanced at Kaban.

"Jalair has great interest in hawks," Kaban said. "Though he says he has never trained any, I find him speaking with authority on the subject."

Jalair remembered how Kaban had questioned him on hawking after seeing Dhuvik's carved horn.

"Would you like to spend your time hawking, Jalair?" the Khan asked him.

"Yes," Jalair answered, wondering if the Khan meant to make sport of him.

The Khan glanced around the *yurt*. "Idikut! Will you test this boy's feeling for hawks?"

Idikut came out of the shadows. He did not wear breastplates, but a sky blue cloak lined with white silk hung from his shoulders. On the back, Jalair saw when Idikut bowed, was embroidered in silver thread the likeness of a gyrfalcon, tapered wings thrust out as the hawk seemingly hung in the air. The falconer's purse, used to carry spare gear, was fastened to Idikut's broad leather belt.

"I will test the boy gladly," Idikut smiled. "He can begin tomorrow by cleaning out the mews."

"Idikut is the Master of Hawking," the Khan explained to Jalair. "Report to him tomorrow to begin your testing. I hope he finds you a suitable worker."

"And so do I," the Master of Hawking laughed. "The

trade festival is less than two months off, and I will need all the assistance in the mews I can find!"

"Is it really true?" Jalair asked in a daze. "Am I to work with hawks?"

"Yes, if you prove yourself fit for the work." The Khan smiled.

Kaban and the boys bowed as the audience came to an end.

Just as Jalair turned to follow them out, a familiar object caught his eye.

A leather pouch, such as the Khan's messengers used, lay carelessly on a nearby cushion. The flap was open, and protruding from the pouch was the pointed end of a horn. No part of the design showed, but Jalair had worked too hard and long not to recognize the drinking horn he had carved for Dhuvik.

"Come, Jalair!" Dhuvik muttered, pulling him by the sleeve.

Outside, they reclaimed their weapons and mounted. Kaban trotted ahead of the boys, returning the greetings of friends who welcomed him home.

"Where are we going?" Jalair asked.

"Home," said Dhuvik. "You are to live with us."

Kaban's *yurt* was close to the river, and the domed tent was brightly painted with horses and battle scenes. Jalair remembered Dhuvik telling him that Kaban was an officer of the army who had fought in many battles before leading caravans to the west.

A woman in beautiful, colored silks, her highly piled hair sparkling with diamonds and rubies, came from the *yurt* to greet them as Kaban's servants took their horses. Jalair realized this was Chentai, Dhuvik's mother, of whom his friend had spoken many times.

Chentai embraced Kaban, then Dhuvik, and when they explained Jalair was to live with them, she said, "I am proud and happy to have another son. Welcome home, Jalair." Her eyes were warm and smiling, and Jalair found himself liking her very much.

"And now we must have the welcoming feast!" Chentai exclaimed happily as they entered the *yurt*. "Kaban, I gave orders for a great banquet when I heard the report of your return."

"Will our friends and neighbors join us in the feasting?" Kaban asked.

Chentai laughed. "Oh, yes! I invited everyone. Now, hurry. There are bowls of hot water ready for your baths."

Kaban's *yurt* was made in the same way as the smaller one used on the trail. Heavy curtains formed small sleeping rooms on one side. The sloping walls were covered with Kaban's armor and weapons. In the center, beneath the smoke hole, was a fire surrounded by embroidered cushions, platters of delicacies, and drinking horns in their stands. Even now, Kaban's servants hurried back and forth, setting out more cushions and bowls of food.

Dhuvik took Jalair into one of the small rooms formed at the side of the *yurt* by curtains. "This is where I sleep, and now it is your room too."

"But where do the servants stay?" Jalair asked.

"They have a *yurt* of their own, right in back of ours." Dhuvik opened a brightly painted chest and began laying out new clothes for himself and Jalair. "Hurry, the guests will soon be here."

They bathed quickly and changed to fresh clothes. Through the thick curtain, Jalair could hear visitors arriving. When the boys entered the main room, it was to greet a crowd of armored warriors, gayly dressed women, and boys eager with questions about the western world.

"Come here, Jalair," Kaban called to him.

A little uneasy over the show of arms and armor the warriors bore, Jalair went to Kaban. Dhuvik's father had changed from trail clothes to shining plate armor. A leopard skin cloak, brought from Tibet, fell from his shoulders. Gone was the stern expression of a caravan leader, and in its place the smile of a man glad to be home with friends and family.

"This is Jalair," Kaban announced to the crowd. "He has come to live with us."

"We heard the news," a warrior said, the yellow dragon painted on his armor snarling in the firelight. "And we have brought luck gifts to the new member of the family."

This seemed to be a signal, for Jalair was at once surrounded by laughing warriors, their smiling wives and joking sons. They pressed their gifts into his arms. Belts of silver, of leather, of carved wooden plates. Cloaks and boots, and richly decorated caps and mittens. A firestriker from Cathay. Horsewhips, bows, quivers of arrows. Someone even gave him a saddle and bridle.

Jalair protested that he could not accept these fine things, but they only laughed.

"You must keep them." Dhuvik grinned. "They are luck gifts, which are given to every new member of a family."

Someone struck up a lute, and then everyone began singing as servants passed around horns of milk, and of wine made of rice and dates. Soon the gong was struck, and the feast began. All sat on cushions around the fire, taking what meats, rice, cheese, and fruits they wished from the servants.

Jalair sat among the other boys, listening to them talk about the new class to begin the following week at the officers' school.

Things had happened so quickly! Only that morning the caravan had arrived in Karakorum. Now Jalair sat in Kaban's *yurt*, counted as one of his sons. Was it possible Kaban had some purpose of his own in thus keeping Jalair under his eye? He glanced at Dhuvik's father, laughing and talking with his friends. It hardly seemed Kaban would lay secret traps, so direct and honest was he. Yet there was the matter of the carved horn, left lying in the *yurt* of Genghis Khan.

Jalair burned to ask Dhuvik why the horn had been sent to the Khan. If only there were a way of finding out without arousing suspicion. He began to think out the words he might use.

Gradually, the feasting ended, and once more the lute was struck. "Chentai, Chentai! A song." Others took up the cry until at last, smiling, Chentai reached for the lute. Cradling it in her lap, she struck a chord, and the *yurt* fell into silence.

Chentai sang the long epic of the Blue Wolf, legendary ancestor of the Mongols, and how the Blue Wolf helped the Brave People become a strong and courageous tribe. The notes of the ancient lay rang out clearly, and Jalair closed his eyes, for a picture had formed in his mind.

There was sunshine, laughter, and a woman singing—all mixed together. And a strong-looking man leaned over the woman's shoulder, smiling as she sang. Darien and Irian.

The song ended, and so did the picture in Jalair's mind.

Then the lutes, drums, and flutes struck up and spun madly together. With a shout, a warrior sprang up and began stamping his booted feet. Soon everyone joined the dancing, and colorful figures whirled around the fire.

The celebration lasted all afternoon, ending only after nightfall. When the last guest departed, Kaban looked a long moment at his family. "It is good to be home," he said.

"Come, Jalair." Dhuvik tugged his sleeve. "You must be up early tomorrow to begin your work with Idikut."

Servants had made up a bed for Jalair in Dhuvik's sleeping quarters. Both boys were glad to retire, for the day had been a long one.

"Dhuvik," Jalair said after they had settled down and the oil lamp had been put out. "During the feast you did not use the horn I carved for you."

"Oh, father said he showed it to the Khan, for the carving was well done."

"Then the Khan still has it?" Jalair remembered too clearly the horn lying on the cushion in the great white *yurt*.

"Yes," Dhuvik said, yawning. "He wanted to keep it for a while. Perhaps he plans to have copies made for his court."

Perhaps, Jalair thought. And perhaps not.

The next morning, a servant awoke Jalair, brought him washing water, and laid his breakfast before silently departing. Jalair ate alone in the main room of the *yurt*, for a hawker's work began while others still slept.

The servant entered to clear away the empty dishes. "Your horse is ready, young master," the man said.

"I do not know where Idikut, the Master of Hawking, is to be found," Jalair said uncertainly.

"The mews is on the edge of Karakorum," the servant replied. He gave directions, then Jalair left, trotting through the silent city. Smoke rising from *yurts* here and there told of other early risers. Far out on the plains surrounding

Karakorum, Jalair saw the dark masses of the herds—yaks, camels, horses, and sheep.

The mews was easy to find, for this *yurt* that housed the Khan's hawks was brightly painted with hunting scenes. Jalair picketed his horse near the entrance, then stepped through the *yurt's* low doorway.

The first thing he saw was Idikut's bright blue cloak with its embroidered silver gyrfalcon. The Hawk Master was bending over a hooded goshawk, one of many hawks tethered to the bar perches running along the walls of the *yurt*. He glanced up, and greeted Jalair heartily. "Before you can work, Jalair, you must know the mews. Where is your horse?"

"Outside."

"Come with me. There is a corral in back where I keep my own mount."

Following Idikut, Jalair unsaddled his horse and turned it loose in the small corral attached to the mews. Then Idikut took him over every inch of his domain. Jalair saw that the mews was not one *yurt*, but three.

The three *yurts* were set in a row, their low doorways touching. The first one, with a second doorway leading outside, was the *yurt* for fully trained hawks. The second *yurt* contained all the gear used in training hawks. The third *yurt* was called the hack room, where newly-caught hawks learned their first lessons in submitting to man.

Behind the three connected *yurts* were two areas fenced in with felt stretched on poles. One was the lure ring, where hawks learned to hunt, and the other was the weathering ring where hawks could sit in the sun and fresh air. Beyond the two rings was the small circular corral.

But of all the parts of the mews, Jalair was most fascinated with the hawk room. Here were the hunters, standing patiently on their perches, sharp eyes hooded and feet leashed. Occasionally a hawk stretched his wings in great slow beats, and Jalair's heart thumped as he pictured the bird climbing to its pitch in the sky.

"Well, you certainly have a liking for hawks," Idikut said, startling Jalair out of his absorbed study. "But let us see if you also have a liking for work."

"It matters not what I do," Jalair said eagerly, "as long as I can be near the hawks." Near enough to study and handle peregrines, goshawks, lanners, sakers, gyrfalcons—the nobility of the skies!

Jalair came to like Idikut more and more as the morning passed. Together they cleaned the mews, fed and watered the hawks, while the Master relentlessly rapped questions at Jalair. Noon came, and Idikut invited Jalair to share his lunch of cheese and cold meat.

"Where did you learn so much of hawking?" Idikut asked.

"In the market places, the streets, the parks. Wherever I saw men with hawks."

That afternoon, Idikut set him to making leather hoods. The hours passed quickly and happily for Jalair. He liked the blue-cloaked Hawk Master who was quick to praise and patient in instructing. It was only as Jalair left after the day's work that he remembered something was missing.

He had seen nothing of the Golden Hawks.

On his various errands throughout the day, Jalair had been to every part of the mews. Yet he had not seen a hawk that he could not identify as one of the wild species.

He frowned as he trotted back to Kaban's *yurt*. Karakorum was the city of Genghis Khan. The Golden Hawks had to be here.

Jalair resolved to keep his ears open for any mention of Darien's great hunters.

The week sped by—a glorious week for Jalair who was surrounded by hawks of all kinds, working at the side of a man who knew and understood them. Before he realized it, he and Idikut became firm friends. The Hawk Master guided Jalair's efforts with friendly patience, encouraging his inexperienced hands at every task from repairing gear to handling the Khan's prize hawks.

"Truly," grinned Idikut at the end of the week, "I know not how I managed the mews without you, Jalair."

"Were there no other boys to help you before I came?"

"Often some boys passed their time in the mews and gave me a little help," Idikut answered. "Yet they were eager to enter the officers' school or join the army." The Hawk Master rested his hand on Jalair's shoulder. "It is a great and rare

thing when a boy has a hawker's heart." He turned abruptly, going to one of the perches. He returned with a young hooded peregrine which he placed in Jalair's hands. "Here, boy," he said gruffly. "Make your mistakes on your own hawk. Then you will know better when you handle the Khan's birds."

Jalair felt the beating heart of the young bird in his hands. It was a falcon, that is, a female. Falcons were better hunters than the tiercels, the males. Her feathers were stiff and sleek, and he knew this hawk would be as fast as an arrow shot from the sun.

"My own hawk, Idikut?" He stared at the hunter in his hands, at her blue back and speckled white breast. Though she was still young and untrained, Jalair could almost feel the power and fearlessness of the hawk that was his.

"Now don't spend all your time with it," Idikut laughed. "In two weeks' time we are to go hawking with the Khan. Meanwhile, you have much to learn."

Jalair scarcely heard him.

His first hawk—a peregrine falcon. His very own!

And truly, it seemed finer than the Golden Hawks he had never seen.

7 Master of the Golden Hawks

That evening Jalair galloped from the mews on the edge of the city to the *yurt* of Kaban. Tossing the reins to a servant, he burst inside, shouting with excitement.

Chentai, Dhuvik, and Kaban were already seated, waiting for Jalair to join them before beginning the evening meal. Laughing, Chentai pulled Jalair to a cushion. "You must not talk until you can breathe again," she teased.

Jalair waited until he got his breath back, then told them about the peregrine falcon Idikut had given him. "It is mine—my very own hawk! I am going to call her Arrow, and she will be the finest hunter in the empire."

"Then you have passed the test," Kaban said with a smile.

When Jalair looked up in surprise, Kaban added, "You remember that the Khan said you could be a hawker only if you proved worthy of the task. Now we know you are, for Idikut does not readily give away fine hawks, especially falcons."

Jalair had forgotten all about the trial period. The past week he had felt so much at home in the mews that he might have been hawking all his life. He remembered Samarkand now, and Kurush, and the stranger from Urgendj who had come to take him to Shah Ala-u-Din's court where Jalair would never have handled a hawk himself. How far away Khoresm seemed!

But Dhuvik's eager words snatched his thoughts away from his distant homeland.

"Look, Jalair!" Dhuvik jumped up and brought over a new helmet. It was of leather, covered with plates of steel, very much like the helmet Kaban wore on the caravan trail. But Dhuvik's had a nail-studded leather flap to protect the back of his neck. And instead of the white horsetail crest that marked Kaban's rank, there flowed from Dhuvik's a crest of red. "Tomorrow the new student officers' class begins, and today I went over for my helmet. The red crest is the mark of the cadet." His dark eyes shone with pride. "In our second year, we will be given finer swords than those we use now. Yatu, who teaches dueling, says we first must learn to use a sword properly before we get the better weapons."

"I would not know what to do with a sword," Jalair said. "But I know what I am doing when I help Idikut with the hawks."

"I would rather train for the army," Dhuvik said cheerfully. "But there is one thing I do not care for. We cadets must learn to read and write, and I have no patience for a scholar's work."

"But you will study hard, Dhuvik," Kaban said sternly. "You know what will happen if you fail."

"What would happen?" Jalair asked.

"Courage is not enough to be an officer," Kaban said. "The Khan demands wisdom among his leaders as well. Boys who fail in their studies become regular soldiers in the ranks, along with the boys who did not attend the school at all."

"How long must you study, Dhuvik?" Jalair asked.

"Five years," Dhuvik answered. "But before any boy is admitted to the school, he must spend one year as an army messenger. Besides reading and writing, we must learn either Cathayan or Arabic, and geography, battle tactics, and government."

"Do you learn to use every weapon?" Jalair asked.

"Oh, yes! That is the best part. Spear, bow, crossbow, and sword. Some boys will specialize in artillery—stone casters, catapults, and battering rams. And of course, we are all expert horsemen. At graduation, the best students are chosen for the Khan's personal guard."

"That reminds me," Jalair said with deliberate casualness. "The Khan is going hawking two weeks from now, and I am to come along to help."

"Ah, an honor indeed!" Chentai exclaimed happily. "I am glad my sons are well settled in their careers."

"You will find the Khan an expert hawker," Kaban added.

"He is the best warrior, too," Dhuvik said.

"Does Genghis Khan do everything better than anyone else?" Jalair asked.

"Of course," Dhuvik said, reaching for a second helping of rice. "Otherwise he would not be khan."

After the meal, Kaban suggested Chentai sing them one

of the traditional lays. She clapped her hands for the lute, and cradling it, asked them what song they would have.

"A tale of the caravan routes," Kaban said.

"A battle song!" cried Dhuvik.

Chentai smiled. "You have heard them before, but I think Jalair would like to hear the story of a great hawk hunt." So saying, she strummed the lute and sang of hardy riders galloping through the tall steppe grass beneath their hawks.

To Jalair it sounded like the description of his private dream land. Dreamily listening to Chentai's voice, he thought that surely the mother he could not remember must have sung to him in like fashion.

On the day the Khan was to go hawking, Jalair went to the mews an hour earlier than usual as Idikut bade him. Jalair was a little apprehensive at the thought of handling hawks under the eye of Genghis Khan. But he remembered how Idikut had praised him for his work, and felt a little reassured.

For the past two weeks, Jalair had worked long and hard with the Hawk Master, eagerly absorbing the many details Idikut taught him.

There were many hawks of many breeds in various stages of their training. Jalair learned to feed the hawks still at hack, proud that Idikut would trust him with such important work. Unhacked birds were still wild, and were kept and fed in total darkness. They had to go through this stage of their training in order to learn to trust mankind. The hawker had to be at once gentle and firm with the birds, spending much time in the dark hack room stroking them and talking their fears away.

Other hawks were being manned, that is, taken around through the city while leashed to the fist, and occasionally having their hoods removed. This was done so the hawk could become accustomed to the noises and sights of man and his possessions. Thus, when unhooded in the field, the hawk would not be confused by strange sights and sounds. Once the hawks were manned, they had to be lured.

Jalair made lures by padding a piece of iron and tying feathers and pieces of meat to it. This he swung around his

head on a long rope in the lure ring. Idikut would unhood the hawks one at a time, and the birds attempted to strike down the lure as if it were live quarry.

Lured hawks were taken out on the plains surrounding Karakorum and hooded off to fly at captured birds Idikut or Jalair released for them. Hawks who had already learned this phase of hunting were flown regularly every second day, to seek out their own prey while Idikut and Jalair galloped beneath them to start up game.

Occasionally on these trips to the plains, they would meet one or two other men in the field with their hawks. Jalair was surprised until Idikut told him, "I care only for the Khan's hawks and some of the highest generals' birds. Others who hawk either train their own or employ a man to do this work, though many owners come to me for advice."

Jalair learned also how to care for ill hawks, and the few kept over from last year which were now molting.

Everything was so new, so exciting, that memories of Khoresm faded rapidly in Jalair's happiness of working with hawks. When he did think of Kurush and the stranger from Ugendj, it was with a guilty twinge that he quickly brushed aside.

In the evenings, Jalair would come home content. He

passed many pleasant hours with his Mongol family. Chentai often sang the old songs, Kaban would tell of great battles in which he had fought, and Dhuvik would describe the day's happenings at school. Jalair would tell of his work in the mews, for everyone seemed interested in his activities.

Now it was the day for the Khan's hunt, and Jalair hoped he would make no mistakes.

The Hawk Master carefully selected the very best hunters, and Jalair fitted them with hoods crested with a tuft of feathers. The jesses, the straps permanently fastened to a hawk's legs, were changed from ordinary leather straps to highly decorated ones, in honor of the Khan. A pair of jesses consisted of two leather straps tied to a metal ring. Jalair carefully tied the free ends to the hawk's legs, and slipped the leash through the jess ring. Then he tied the leash to the top bar of the field cadge.

The field cadge was a rectangular frame of smooth wood on which the hawks could perch comfortably. There were four legs, one at each corner, which permitted the hawker to set the cadge on the ground, or to hold it while riding to the field.

"Hurry, Jalair," Idikut urged as he fashioned lures to recover runaway hawks. "You must pack the field kit."

Jalair took a leather bag and filled it with cooked chicken legs and pieces of boiled meat. A hawk is never permitted to feed from its catch, but must still be rewarded with food for its work. Another bag was packed with spare jesses, gauntlets, hoods, bells, and other equipment.

"Help me file these talons." Idikut handed Jalair a pumice stone, and they both squatted near the field cadge.

They went to work quickly and silently. Jalair gently lifted each hawk's foot in turn and smoothed off the sharp points of the claws. This was done so the birds would not pierce the leather gauntlets, or become tangled in their jesses. Jalair was so busy he hardly noticed someone entering the mews.

"Are the hawks ready, Idikut?" asked a deep voice.

Jalair released the last hawk's foot and turned around. Genghis Khan stepped over to appraise the chosen hawks, and he nodded to Jalair.

"Ready and eager for the chase, my Khan," Idikut answered.

Jalair busied himself with gathering up the field kits and other gear to be taken along. He hardly knew how to act in the presence of Genghis Khan. Idikut went on with his work after giving the Khan no more than a token bow. This was quite different from the formality of the Khan's court.

"Jalair, get our horses," Idikut said.

"No need," the Khan said, turning from the hawks on the cadge. "I had them brought up to save time." The Khan cooly studied Jalair from head to foot. "Idikut, does this boy have a hawker's heart?"

"In truth, my Khan," the Hawk Master replied, slipping his right arm beneath the cadge and lifting it, "Jalair might have been a hawk himself to so understand the birds."

A quick smile flashed across the stern features. "Well, we shall see how he does in the field," the Khan answered.

Four horsemen awaited them outside. One had dismounted to hold the Khan's mount. Their gold horsetail crests told of their general's rank. Jalair was introduced to them, and he recognized the names of Soo, Chepe Noyon, Bayan, and Subotai. These great generals were also Dhuvik's military instructors until such a time as war might take them from these peaceful tasks.

Jalair fastened the field kits to his saddle and mounted. Idikut would trust no one but himself to carry the hawks, and Jalair marveled at the ease with which the Hawk Master mounted while holding the clumsy cadge.

"Where is the field, Idikut?" Bayan asked as they trotted clear of the last few *yurts* on the edge of Karakorum.

"Two miles to the northeast," the Hawk Master replied, carefully holding the cadge in front of him. "The plain stretches into a pair of ridges, and we can have both woodland and field hunting today. Subotai, I have brought your favorite goshawk."

"And it will best Chepe's tattered old peregrine," the general grinned.

Chepe Noyon roared out a denial. "My jeweled sword to you, Subotai, if your molting slow-winged crow catches a larger prey than my fine per!"

"Done!" cried Subotai. "A shield to you if you win, though that is indeed a wild thought."

Bayan laughed. "Gold-linked belts to you both if my hawk does not catch more prey than either of your birds."

"You are a generous man, Bayan," Soo replied with a grin. "And I will match your offer, for my gyrfalcon will surely show up as the best hunter today."

"A silver-mounted saddle to the best hawker," smiled the Khan, pleased with the keen competition.

"And the poorest hawker, my Khan?" asked Chepe. "What shall be his penalty?"

"Do not ask for a penalty for yourself, Chepe," Soo advised.

Jalair laughed at the bantering of the generals. His fears that he might make some terrible mistake soon melted in their jokes and challenges.

When they reached the place selected by Idikut, Jalair dismounted and handed a gauntlet to each of the hawkers. Idikut placed the cadge on the ground, and Jalair slipped thin leather straps over the necks of the hawks. These thongs would be used to catapult the hawk quickly into the air. The Hawk Master untied each bird and handed it up to its mounted owner. Bells tinkled as the hawks found good foothold on the gauntleted fists.

"Who shall be first to try for the Khan's prize?" Soo asked, stroking his gyrfalcon.

"I am not afraid to try my hawk's wings," Chepe declared boldly.

"Jalair, begin from the north end of the field and drive the game toward us," Idikut said.

Jalair mounted and trotted to the far end of the field. He waited, watching Chepe Noyon slip the hood from his peregrine. Taking in the slack of the neck thong, Chepe pulled his hawk into a horizontal position, then, drawing back his arms, he flung the peregrine into the air. The falcon, for the per was a female, beat her long pointed wings slowly and powerfully, planing upward in a spiral. When she reached her pitch, she waited on, drifting in a watchful circle.

Jalair studied the falcon's slate-blue back as the per dipped and circled, and the morning sun seemed to redden her white breast. He could just hear the faint tinkle of the bells on her legs in spite of her height, for the sound could be heard a long way off.

He nudged his horse into motion and began a leisurely canter down the field through the tall steppe grass. Ahead of his horse, the grass suddenly moved as a hare darted from its hiding place. Jalair pulled his horse down to a trot to allow the waiting peregrine more room for her plunge.

Above, the falcon paused in her circling, then suddenly stroked her great wings downward and snapped them to her sides. Head first, the per plunged down, faster and faster until she was only a blue blur in the lighter blue sky. Jalair saw the waving grass line zig-zag frantically as the hare, sensing the danger, twisted away from his enemy. The falcon changed her direction with an action-blurred stroke of her mighty wings.

Then suddenly, those wings shot out as the per closed with the ground. Out thrust the fatal talons and wings beat frantically, checking her speed, and she dealt the final blow with closed fist.

Jalair dismounted and walked over. The peregrine stood off from her prey, quietly smoothing her feathers. Gently he lifted her to his gauntleted fist. When Chepe Noyon's piercing whistle shrilled across the plain, Jalair tossed the falcon off to fly back to her master. There, Chepe Noyon would reward her with a bit of meat from the field kit. Picking up the fallen hare, Jalair put it in a sling tied to his pommel. The quarry was unmarked, since most hawks used in hunting kill with a stout blow of the closed fist.

Jalair signaled a successful kill, and trotted back to his position.

Then it was Soo's turn to slip his hawk. Hooded off, the gyrfalcon ringed up and waited on, her gray wings silvery in the sun, and the dark breast bars showing clearly.

This time Jalair flushed a partridge. The bird fluttered frantically before it sensed the speeding gray hunter stooping down from above. The partridge went to ground, but the gyr never hesitated. There was a quick upbeat of wings, a stroke from the closed fist, and the grass stilled.

The morning passed quickly. When his game bag was filled, Jalair returned to the hawkers to show them their quarry. The hawks were allowed to rest, then Jalair began driving up between the ridges, where the woodlands provided the best hunting for the goshawks.

Bayan's goshawk was a haggard. This meant it had been a fully matured adult when caught for training. Such birds never entirely lose their wildness, though they hunt with a dash and spirit seldom equaled in branchers—hawks caught and trained before they were a year old. Bayan's black-backed and gray-breasted goshawk became confused and excited at the sight of her old home grounds. Several times the haggard checked, leaving her initial quarry in favor of another. Twice she raked away, and only Idikut's patience and skill lured the falcon back to the fist. Finally, she brought down an excellent large squirrel.

Genghis Khan's gyrfalcon was a tiercel, a male. Usually tiercels do not hunt as well as falcons, but this gyr proved a better bird than Soo's. The Khan's gyrfalcon was of the white northern variety, far superior to the darker birds of the south.

"A good hunt," Subotai said, glancing at the full game bags. "Idikut, when can we fly in casts?"

"Not for some time," the Hawk Master replied. "It takes a long time to train hawks to hunt in pairs. But I will have several casts ready for the hawk trials at the festival next month."

"Good," cried Chepe Noyon. "I know where I can purchase matched sakers, and you will help me win the cast competition, Idikut."

"Only if they are branchers," the Hawk Master replied. "The haggards are too wild to begin training now."

"These sakers are branchers," Chepe said. "I will bring the pair to you tomorrow."

"And you, Jalair," the Khan said, turning to him. "Will you also enter the hawk meet? There is a division for boys your age."

This was the first Jalair knew of a hawking competition, though he had heard talk of the festival to come a month

hence. "I would like to enter," he said. "But I have only just begun training the brancher peregrine falcon Idikut gave me. Her name is Arrow."

"A lad with a hawker's heart can make up the lack of time." The Khan smiled. "Be sure to enter, Jalair."

Jalair needed little urging to display his hawking skill. "Then I will enter." He grinned.

Idikut took the men's hawks and leashed them to the cadge while Jalair gathered the gear they had used.

The Khan and his four spirited generals quickly agreed on a race back to Karakorum, and, shouting farewell to Idikut and Jalair, spurred their mounts across the grassy plain, cloaks flying in the wind.

"The hunt was more fun that I thought it would be," said Jalair, tying the field kits to his saddle. "In Samarkand, a boy must always be polite and quiet before his elders. But here, he can laugh and shout and gallop on his horse."

Idikut smiled. "There will be many hunts. But you have hard work ahead of you if you would be a hawker."

"This is play, not work." Jalair laughed.

Mounting, they set out at a leisurely trot toward Karakorum. Idikut decided to approach the city from a different direction, for the wind must be kept at his back as he held the cadge in front of him. Otherwise the hawks' feathers would be ruffled, and perhaps damaged.

As they circled the distant city, Jalair saw a bright flash in the sky. Beneath it was a horseman. "Look, Idikut!"

"That is Yatu," the Hawk Master said. "We will pass near him."

They trotted closer, Jalair hardly able to keep his eyes from the hawk ringing above. Idikut hailed the horseman, who also held a cadge before him on his saddle. On it were sitting two hooded hawks—a falcon and a tiercel. They were the same color, for the only difference between female and male was the falcon's larger size. Jalair let his reins drop as he turned his face once more to the sky and stared at the third hawk, a tiercel, which was still circling overhead.

The wings were the color of the sun, and the breast was touched with the hue of burnished copper. The hawk was larger than a peregrine, and his wait-on was smooth and alert as he seemingly turned on the tip of his long, pointed wing.

"The hawk can fly higher than that," said Yatu, grinning at Jalair's astonishment. "And you should see him stoop! These are the finest hawks in the world, and, fittingly enough, only Genghis Khan may own them."

Called back to earth, Jalair felt foolish for staring so earnestly. He greeted Yatu warmly, for Chentai had sung many battle songs telling of the warrior's courage.

"Dhuvik talks of you all the time," Jalair said. "And Kaban says you are one of the finest warriors in the empire."

Yatu laughed. "No longer, Jalair. Now I sit by the fires and tell stories to boys your age."

But Jalair knew Yatu could still give good account of himself in any battle. He studied the warrior as Idikut and Yatu discussed hawks.

Yatu's hands, as he stroked the hooded hawks on the cadge, told of power and strength, yet their touch was gentle. A long scar reached from Yatu's left ear down across his jaw, but his eyes held a glint of humor as if he had never seen the confusion and alarms of the battlefield. The engraving on the hilt of his sword was almost worn away from use. Jalair was glad Yatu was no enemy of his.

"Come, Jalair," Idikut said. "We must take our hawks to the mews."

Jalair opened his mouth to ask about Yatu's magnificent hawks, but already Idikut had called his farewell and turned his horse away. Jalair hastily said good-by and followed the Hawk Master.

"What hawks were those?" Jalair asked him excitedly. "Their flight makes a peregrine look like a sparrow. Do you think Yatu would let us fly them sometime?"

"We can never fly them, Jalair, for they are the Golden Hawks."

The Golden Hawks!

Jalair turned in his saddle, and the flash of golden wings above Yatu opened an old wound in his heart. He should have guessed it, for those birds could be none but the Golden Hawks. Often had Kurush recited the old tale in Samarkand. Now he, Jalair, was in the midst of his father's enemies, watching the hawks Darien had created to honor the Shah of Khoresm being flown and handled by a Mongol!

"You are quiet, Jalair." Idikut smiled. "Where are your thousand questions of hawking now?"

"I—I was wondering why the Khan does not fly his Golden Hawks," Jalair stammered.

"The Khan, as a mark of respect, is waiting until the true master of the Goldens returns. Until then, no one shall fly them. Yatu only breeds and cares for them until their master returns."

"And their master?" asked Jalair, his heart thumping against his ribs. Now he would know his father's slayer, for surely the master of the Golden Hawks was the same man who stole them from Darien and gave them to Genghis Khan to further his own prestige. "Who is the master of the Golden Hawks?"

"I cannot say more than his name," Idikut replied. "He is called Torgul."

And then thoughts of the Golden Hawks, the killing

of Darien, the enslaving of Irian were driven from Jalair's mind.

For the name, "Torgul," had a familiar ring in his ears.
Where was he?
Who was he?

8 Who Is Torgul?

The Golden Hawks were in Karakorum.

Darien's fabulous birds were not a legend or a dream. But if the Golden Hawks were real, so was the manner of Darien's death, the humiliation of Irian's slavery, and the narrow escape of Jalair himself as the last living caravan member galloped away with Jalair in his arms.

The Mongol who committed these crimes was real and alive. His name was Torgul, and somewhere Jalair had heard it before.

The next three days Jalair did his work indifferently at the mews as he struggled to remember Torgul and call up the face of Darien's slayer. The half-memory nagged him even during his free time, but luckily Dhuvik was so occupied with the new routine of the officers' school that Jalair was spared the necessity of explaining his occasional lapses of attention.

One morning as Jalair entered the mews, he stopped in horror.

The earthen floor was littered with feathers. Among them were the bodies of five hawks. One of these, Jalair saw with a sinking feeling, was the Khan's best gyrfalcon. Raw scratches scarred the places on the perch bars where the five had been tethered. Broken leashes, clawed apart, hung in limp confusion. Idikut, the blue Hawk Master's cloak hanging from his brooding shoulders, was silently untying a sixth dead hawk that dangled by its leash from the perch.

"What happened?" Jalair cried.

Idikut pointed to a sack on the floor, its contents bulging and thumping. "That goshawk tore loose during the night and slaughtered six hawks. I shall have to put it out of the way for a few days until it calms down."

"Whose is it?"

"Bayan's."

Jalair remembered now. It was the haggard, trained but still half-wild. "And Bayan was so proud of her, too," he said.

"It was not the haggard's fault," Idikut replied. "Nor even Bayan's. Come here, Jalair."

Idikut pointed to the place where Bayan's goshawk had been tethered the night before. The Hawk Master picked up the leash still tied to the bar and pulled steadily until the leather snapped. "An old and brittle leash," Idikut said. "Feel it. It is stiff, and there are two or three places where it is cracked across."

There was no need for Jalair to feel the old leash. He had known it was frayed when he tethered the goshawk the night before. "It was the last one on hand," he said, not daring to look at Idikut.

"You should have made a new one," Idikut said firmly.

"I thought it would make no great difference even if the goshawk did get loose," Jalair said in a low voice. "The hawks are always hooded in the mews, and well fed."

"Jalair, a goshawk is often called a mews killer," the Hawk Master said more gently. "They are fierce hunters, as you know. If one can work its way loose, even hooded, it will attack the other birds. This is true even if the goshawk is well fed, which this one was."

Jalair stared at the wreckage on the floor. It was all his fault.

Idikut put a hand on his shoulder. "It is a serious thing, Jalair. But not that serious. You did not know about killer goshawks before, but now you do. I do not think you will ever forget this lesson."

Jalair shook his head. "No, I will never forget."

"Very well." Idikut spoke more cheerfully. "Now help me clean the mews."

"But what about the Khan's white gyrfalcon?" Jalair pictured himself standing stiffly before the Khan's carved throne, trying to explain while the fierce gray eyes bored into him.

"That matters little," Idikut said casually. "Accidents do happen to hawks. Besides, you know we must release almost all the hawks in time for the fall migration. Next spring, as always, new hawks will be caught and trained."

"I suppose I will not be allowed to handle the hawks after this," Jalair said miserably.

"Why not?" Idikut said, managing a grin. "How can you

be a hawker if you do not learn?" Within an hour, Idikut seemed to dismiss the entire incident.

Jalair resolved to forget about Torgul and keep his mind on his work. It was trying to remember why he seemed to know the name that had made him careless in his duties. He could learn about Torgul in other ways.

That evening as he rode home, he saw a flash of gold in the sky. Yatu was out with some of the Golden Hawks. It gave Jalair an idea.

During the evening meal, Jalair casually mentioned seeing the Golden Hawks. "Idikut says Yatu is only caring for them until Torgul comes back. Torgul is really their master." He stopped, waiting for someone to begin talking of the master of the Goldens.

"True enough," said Kaban. "Torgul is master of the Golden Hawks."

There was just a moment of silence, and then Chentai began describing the visit she had made to her sister that afternoon.

Jalair was astonished. His Mongol family had always been eager to discuss any subject at all. Where now were their exuberant explanations, stories, and descriptions? The name of the honored Torgul was greeted only with silence.

It made him a little uneasy.

As the days went by, Jalair paid more attention to his work and soon became absorbed in it. He was busily training Arrow now, arising an hour earlier so it would not interfere with his duties in the mews. Idikut often came earlier too, and gave advice that Jalair welcomed.

As Dhuvik became accustomed to his school routine, he found more free time to spend with Jalair. After the day's work, the boys raced on the plains, or wandered through the city talking to friends. Jalair was surprised when many Mongols recognized him and asked after the hawks. Once, a friend of Kaban's invited the boys into his *yurt*, and asked Jalair's advice about his saker falcon.

Often they rode out beyond the herds with Arrow. Dhuvik would swing the lure while Jalair slipped the peregrine after it. And Dhuvik delighted in showing Jalair how to use the sword and the lance.

One day after a mock combat, which Jalair lost to Dhuvik's greater skill, Dhuvik said he wanted to learn Turki. "Will you teach me, Jalair?" he asked.

"But why do you want to know it? I thought you had trouble enough with your studies."

"Just with reading and writing," Dhuvik replied. "Learning a language is different. I want to know Turki because Khoresm is our neighboring empire. Already we trade there, and it will not be long before the two empires are close friends. I like the west, and perhaps the Khan will send me there on missions when I am an officer. What is Turki for horse?"

Jalair told him, and so Dhuvik began his lessons.

In this manner, the days passed quickly and pleasantly. Occasionally Jalair thought of Torgul, but not once had he heard anyone speaking of the Master of the Golden Hawks. Nor would he ask questions. Someone might pounce on Jalair's interest in Torgul, just as Kaban had fastened on the design he carved on Dhuvik's drinking horn.

"Our class is having maneuvers tomorrow," Dhuvik announced one night as the family sat around the evening fire in Kaban's *yurt*. "Will you come to watch us, father?"

Kaban shook his head. "The Khan wishes four great caravans to be sent off to Khoresm on the day of the festival. Tomorrow I must leave Karakorum for a few days to make all the arrangements."

"Then perhaps Jalair can watch me," Dhuvik said. "Will you come?"

"If Idikut will let me," Jalair answered.

"If he does, then perhaps you can ride with Yatu to the battlefield," Dhuvik suggested.

The next morning, Idikut allowed Jalair the day free. The young hawker rode to the mews of the Golden Hawks to which Idikut directed him. It was the first time Jalair had seen it.

Like his own mews, it was at the edge of the city. But it consisted of only two connected *yurts* instead of three. The white felt was brightly painted with pictures of Golden Hawks in flight or at rest.

Jalair picketed his horse and stooped through the low

doorway, waiting a moment for his eyes to get accustomed to the gloom. Daylight spilled from the open smoke hole above, and in the darker areas sheep-fat lamps flickered. By this light Jalair saw Yatu moving quietly along the hawks on their perch bars that bent with the curve of the *yurt*. Except for lack of a Hawk Master's cloak, it might have been Idikut examining the Khan's hawks.

Of course, Yatu was only caretaker of the Golden Hawks. Jalair wondered if Torgul wore a special cloak, perhaps a golden one to match the color of the famous hawks he mastered.

Yatu turned and saw Jalair, greeting him cheerfully. "Another moment and you would not have seen me," he said. "I must go to supervise the maneuvers of the youngest class."

"And I would like to go with you, if you will," Jalair said. He explained his invitation from Dhuvik, and Idikut's permission to have the day free.

"Then come along, and welcome." Yatu smiled. "I would show you the mews, but there is little time. This *yurt* is for the older hawks, the other room is used for breeding." Yatu went to fetch his cloak and helmet while Jalair stared in fascination at the hawks his father had created.

Even in the dim light, their golden feathers flashed and sparkled whenever one of the hooded birds shifted restlessly on the perch. This was not often, however, for these birds bore themselves with dignity, not deigning to bicker among themselves as did the hawks in Idikut's mews. Perhaps their noble bearing came from being reared together from the moment of hatching, while other hawks were collected from the wilds and confined in a strange group. That the Golden Hawks could be bred and raised year around in a mews was only one of the many qualities that made them unique among hunting birds.

Yatu returned from the breeding room, wearing his battle cloak and helmet with the white horsetail crest that marked his officer's rank.

Together they rode the long way south of Karakorum, across grassy plains, past the mighty herds, and finally up into the foothills of the mountains ringing the valley.

Yatu stopped on top of a high hill from which Jalair could see easily in every direction. "Watch our battle from here, Jalair. You will not be in the way."

Yatu pointed to a clearing far below, and Jalair now noticed a number of horsemen wearing the red crest of cadet officers. "Dhuvik is in the unit wearing green cloaks. The others have brown cloaks. Take care not to be captured, Jalair." He grinned, spurring his horse and galloping to join the group below.

One of the boys looked up at Yatu's approach, then waved at Jalair. It might have been Dhuvik, but Jalair could not make out features at such a distance.

The boys formed into ranks of their units. Yatu and some other regular army officers gave instructions. Then Jalair saw both units withdraw, marching in opposite directions, trotting along in well-ordered ranks. Soon the two armies disappeared among the tree-covered slopes, but now and then the flash of a red crest showed Jalair where they were.

At last all was quiet beneath the trees. The units were several hills apart, and neither could see the other. Suddenly a whine screamed through the stillness. Jalair jumped, then noticed the flash of an arrow arching through the air. It must be one of the whistling signal arrows of which Dhuvik had spoken. Then a flash of red through the trees showed that at least one of the armies was on the move.

Jalair enjoyed the next two hours. It was fun sitting on a hill watching members of opposite units unknowingly pass each other. One boy in a green cloak dismounted to lead his horse through thick brush and was surprised to find he had walked into a trap of brown-cloaked enemies. Jalair hoped it was not Dhuvik who was taken captive. Once, two groups clashed in the forest, then spilled out to a clearing where they fought it out with dulled dueling swords. Jalair saw to one side a black-crested officer on horseback watching alertly and occasionally calling out to a boy that he was mortally wounded. The "dead" boys had to lie where they were until maneuvers were over. More whistling arrows whined their signals to the hidden units. Once the clash of cymbals heralded the charge of green-cloaks into a camp of brown-clad enemies.

At last the maneuvers were over and the boys were called back to the clearing where they had started. Yatu and the other officers talked briefly, then the boys split into groups and began practicing archery. Leaving the cadets in charge of the other officers, Yatu galloped back to Karakorum, for he could not long leave the Golden Hawks unattended.

But where was Dhuvik? Jalair had expected a wave in his direction from the group below, but none came. Perhaps he had been "killed," and was still lying in the woods, unaware that the mock war was over.

Suddenly Jalair froze. The light breeze that rustled the long grass died, and he could hear someone breathing behind him.

He whirled, and Dhuvik laughed.

Jalair jumped up, relieved, and embarrassed that he was caught so easily. Dhuvik's horse was not far from his own. "How did you manage to come up so quietly?"

Dhuvik laughed again as he sat down on the ground. "That is what we have been learning the last two weeks." He grinned. "We are taught how to keep our horses quiet, too, so we may slip up on enemy sentries if need be. You looked right at me several times, Jalair, but I was hidden just beyond the trees on my way up here."

"Were you 'killed' in the battle?"

Dhuvik shook his head. "But, toward the end, I was 'wounded' in my leg and could not move. So I had to stay where I was until everything was over. It was a bad time for that to happen, for I was just about to capture the captain of the brown unit."

"Who won?"

"The brown unit," Dhuvik shrugged. "Yatu saw how disappointed I was, and he said I could come to visit with you for a while." Then his face brightened. "But Yatu said we all did very well. In fact, we are to give a drill on the afternoon of the trade festival two weeks off."

"The festival! I almost forgot," said Jalair. He had been busy with his work in the mews and with Arrow's training. "Kaban will see you then, Dhuvik."

His friend shook his head. "As you know, the festival marks a year since the trade agreement was signed with Shah

Ala-u-Din of Khoresm. The high point of the celebration will be at noon, when the four richest caravans the world has ever seen will be sent off. Though my father is in charge of all four, he will personally lead the one going to Urgendj. So he will not be here to see the cadets drilling."

Urgendj. That meant Kaban's caravan would go through Samarkand. Perhaps Kaban had other business besides trading Cathay's silk and gems for Persian wine and Oxus Valley cotton.

"Will the other caravans also go to Urgendj?" Jalair asked.

"No, they head for three other Khoresmian cities; Otrar, Meshed, and Kabul. Sending out these rich caravans to four important cities is a fitting way to start the new trade year with Shah Ala-u-Din." He sat up suddenly. "I am glad I am learning Turki, Jalair. For some day we will send ambassadors to Khoresm."

"And you are learning it rapidly," Jalair said.

"Say something in Turki."

Jalair thought a moment, catching his breath as an idea struck him. In Turki, he said, "At the festival, will you drink to the Khan's honor with the carved horn?"

Slowly but accurately Dhuvik answered in the same language. "No, for the Khan still has the horn with him." Then in his own Mongolian, he said, "Did that sound all right, Jalair?"

Jalair nodded absently. "You speak it well."

Genghis Khan still possessed the horn carved with the dangerous design. And Kaban was going to Samarkand!

"Look," called Dhuvik, pointing over the hills that hid Karakorum from their sight.

A tiny gold dot sparkled brilliantly in the sky.

"A Golden Hawk," Dhuvik said. "I did not know they could be seen from such a distance."

"Nor I," said Jalair. "It is because they fly higher than any other hawk. Their golden feathers also make them easy to see from a distance." He hesitated, fearing to display so much interest in the birds that were rightfully his. "Will they be flown during the festival?"

"No," said Dhuvik. "Not unless Torgul returns."

Jalair's heart jumped into his mouth. Did this mean Torgul was expected in Karakorum for the festival? He ached with the unasked question.

But he must be careful not to show interest in Torgul, or to reveal that the name was familiar. Jalair wondered in what hidden camp Torgul had kept Irian a slave—for he knew now there was no slavery among the Mongols. As Kurush had told him, Irian's captor learned from her the name of the child who escaped his arrows. Though there were many named Jalair in Khoresm, there was only one Jalair who escaped, and who knew of the Golden Hawks. And as Kurush often warned, a Mongol's fury would pursue Jalair until some day, inevitably, he would have to face it.

Dhuvik did not notice Jalair's silence, for he was talking eagerly of the festival. "Already people from all over the empire have come to Karakorum, and the streets are filled with merchants and entertainers. Father says there is hardly room for them in the caravansaries and the market place." Dhuvik got to his feet. "I must go back for archery practice."

Jalair remembered to wave farewell as his friend galloped to his class below. He himself rode slowly toward Karakorum, approaching from the southwest where the grass gave way to patches of sand. He passed the familiar stone pillar rising from a ridge of rock that he had noticed the day he arrived in Karakorum.

When he reached the road leading south from the city, he met a Mongol riding in the same direction.

"Now I have some companion for whom to sing," grinned the rider.

Jalair noticed the Mongol was not dressed in armor, but wore only a small sword at his side. Slung on his back was a lute, and now the rider pulled the instrument around and tightened the strings.

"Then you are here for the festival," Jalair said. "Where do you come from?"

"From the banks of the Shilon, a river in the east Gobi," the singer replied, sweeping a chord from his lute.

"The Shilon River men came in about a week ago," Jalair said.

"I set out with the warriors, but I needs must tarry with every lute-singer on the way to exchange songs," the singer replied. "Would you hear of the battle of the Great Wall?" Without waiting for Jalair to reply, the singer lifted his voice in a tale from the Cathayan Wars.

They rode slowly, the better for the minstrel to sing. Jalair's companion swung without pause from one lay to another. But at last he paused to adjust the strings of his lute. "What song will you hear, lad? I know them all, for my father was a singer before me, and his father before him."

This was the moment Jalair had been waiting for. "Sing of Torgul," he said, striving to keep his voice carefree. "And of the Golden Hawks."

The singer hesitated. "That I cannot, lad."

Jalair pretended a lightness he did not feel. "Is it that you do not know *every* song?"

"There is not a song I do not know," the singer replied. "Yet the Khan has ordered the lute-singers to refrain from Torgul's song. The lutes may be struck in Torgul's honor only when he shall return."

"Well then, how could you learn the song?" Jalair asked, wondering if it would be best after all to change the subject entirely.

"Why, the order was not given until two months ago," said the singer, and he named the exact date.

"What reason was given for this order of silence?" Jalair asked. This, then, was why Kaban's family had not spoken of Torgul.

The minstrel laughed. "What reason indeed, except that the Khan has given it? He need not explain his reasons for anything, lad. He is our Khan, wise and courageous, and that is enough for anyone to know."

By now they had reached the city. Nodding farewell, the singer turned his horse down a side street.

Jalair was left alone to puzzle out this latest news. Idikut and Yatu said Genghis Khan honored Torgul, and yet the name of this honored man was forbidden. This order had been a recent one, given on—what day did the singer say?

Jalair had been on the caravan trail then, with Kaban. There was a message sent at Turfan. He calculated rapidly, finding the answer along with a lump in his throat.

The Khan had silenced Torgul's name the very day Kaban's messenger arrived with the carved horn!

Jalair could not begin to guess what was happening. But he knew that now more than ever no one must discover that he was Darien's son.

During the two weeks before the festival, Jalair had little time to ponder the mystery of Torgul's identity. More and more visitors galloped into Karakorum. Granaries were opened to feed the horses, corrals were set up, the caravansaries were filled, and new *yurts* bloomed to house the guests. Some Mongols arrived in family groups, and Jalair often stopped on the way to or from the mews to watch household *yurts* on immense wooden *kibitkas* creaking slowly across the plains, drawn by twenty yoked yaks.

The mews was getting crowded, too. Though Idikut usually cared only for the Khan's birds and those of his generals, the mews was open to all hawkers who were to participate in the hawk trials. Many came to the Hawk Master for advice and help, and soon Jalair found himself another center of questions as Idikut hurried about his work. Arrow was fully trained now, and looking over the birds of visiting boys, Jalair felt he had a good chance to win the hawk meet for his age group.

"What will you ask for if you win the hawk meet?" Dhuvik asked the night before the festival.

Jalair had discovered only yesterday that a winner of any contest could name his own prize. "I know not," he said. "I have been too busy to think about it."

"I am going to ask for a Cathayan crossbow," Dhuvik said. "It has a magazine holding a dozen arrows that can be fired one after the other without reloading."

"What activity is it you will win?" asked Kaban with a smile.

"The lasso competition," Dhuvik said promptly. "And I am going to enter some races, too."

The next morning before dawn, a servant awakened Jalair as he had asked. Hastily gulping down his breakfast, he rode toward the mews.

A silvery dawn cast a cold light over the round *yurts*, humped together as if for warmth. From a few smoke holes struggled the thin smoke strands of breakfast fires lighted for other early risers. In spite of the morning gloom, Jalair saw colored banners flapping in the brisk dawn breeze from *yurts*, wagons, and carts, from standards set in the ground, and from hitching posts.

As he trotted across the city, Jalair remembered the excitement of the last few days when it seemed everyone in Karakorum was busy making flags and ribbons, repainting their *yurts* in bright colors, decorating their wagons and even their animals. Horses' hoofs were painted, and the richer warriors covered their mounts' hoofs with gilt from Cathay. Anything made of metal, from fine weapons to the lowly two-pronged eating fork, was highly polished. Leather saddles, boots, belts, and even food bags were waxed many times until they gleamed.

The immense plain surrounding Karakorum was thick with herds of horses, camels, yaks, and sheep. Only one area to the east had been left clear. It was marked off as the arena for the games and contests.

Even before Jalair reached the mews, the city stirred. Servants emerged and hurried between the *yurts* on their errands. Here and there, artisans, entertainers, and merchants were setting up their stands, for the market place had long since been overcrowded.

In the east the sky flooded with red, and before Jalair's eyes the golden rim of the sun rose from behind the mountains. Suddenly a deep-throated wail floated over the city and echoed among the hills. The horses on the plains lifted their heads.

Startled, Jalair jerked his reins, then remembered that this was the blowing of the gigantic horn brought from Tibet, and it marked the beginning of the festival day.

The great note sounded again, and from the opposite side of Karakorum came a low growl of drums, building and building until it burst into thunder. Then the smash of a hundred cymbals drowned the drums.

Those already abroad in the streets began shouting, for until this moment the silence of the festival day could not be broken. The *yurts* stirred into greater activity, and far off someone began exploding firecrackers. Jalair's heart started to pound with the excitement and color of the festival.

Suddenly he saw two specks of gold circling out on the plain. Yatu was up early.

Then Jalair felt ashamed. Though Darien, Irian, and the Golden Hawks had frequently been in his thoughts, he had been swept along with his work for Idikut, Dhuvik's friendship, and a sense of being part of Kaban's family. Now here he was, in the city of Darien's enemies, ready to enjoy their festival.

He glanced at the *yurts* he was passing. Somewhere in this crowded city he might this day face Torgul.

Brooding, Jalair began to lay his plans.

9 A Prize for the Hawker

The hot sun made the gay banners and painted carts sparkle like the sands of the desert. The streets were crowded, and Jalair, returning from the mews at noon, found his progress slow. Impatiently he nudged his horse through every opening in the celebrating crowd, for Kaban would soon lead the caravans out of the city. Jalair was glad Idikut had allowed him the time to say farewell to Kaban.

All morning the sounds of the festival rang an enticing invitation around the mews. Firecrackers and cymbals, trotting hoofs, barking dogs, shouts of greeting, the cries of children, the merchants calling their wares, and the clank of arms and armor made it hard for Jalair to concentrate on his work.

And work there was!

Jalair was glad to have Yatu there to lend a willing hand when Idikut was too busy to answer the many questions of the warriors who crowded into the mews. Together, the three worked furiously, with hardly time to exchange a word with one another.

Idikut's sky-blue Hawk Master's cloak made him a distinctive figure among the lacquered and mailed warriors. Yatu was resplendent in chain mail and a cloak of bear's skin.

Jalair's own clothes, though new and comfortable, seemed drab compared to the brightness of a city dressed for a festival. He wished that, like Idikut, he too, had some hawker's insignia.

The morning was filled with crises. A flight feather had broken off and had to be spliced together with a wooden pin inside the hollow quill. Excited hawks bated from their perches and tangled their jesses. One broke a claw and was unable to sit on the fist comfortably. Several refused to drink and sulked nervously until Yatu sprayed their wings with water to refresh them. But at last the three hawkers brought order to the confusion of the mews, and finally Idikut gave Jalair time to say farewell to Kaban.

The city's brightness made Jalair blink after the gloom of the mews. Though impatient to reach Kaban's *yurt* in time, he could not help but glance at the jugglers, tumblers, and trained dogs performing wherever they found space. Every warrior rode proudly in his finest armor. Designs painted on breastplates and the colored banners tied below a spear point told the tribe to which the various Mongols belonged.

Merchants, artisans, and entertainers came from every part of the world for the festival. Watching the surge of the crowds was like seeing a parade of countries—Arabia, Cathay, Persia, Tibet. There were ambassadors too, from every province of Genghis Khan's empire—Kara Khitai, Korea, Cathay, and the former country of Hia, known as the Robber Kingdom. Among the city's visitors were Kashgai, Kurd, Khirghize, and even mystics from the strange country of the Hind.

Abruptly, Jalair's horse halted, blocked by two huge carts struggling through the streets. While Jalair waited for them to pass, he heard two voices in the crowd behind him.

"I know not why the Khan desires us to go about the Khoresmian cities without our battle dress," one grumbled. "There might be need of a cross-bow and shield."

"True enough," his companion agreed. "The city governors in the Shah's country are getting more demanding, not being content with our freely given gifts. Instead, they wish to take what they will out of our caravans."

"The robbing of other caravans has made them greedy," replied the first man. "It angers them that we will not let our goods be seized under the guise of gift-giving."

The carts passed, and Jalair rode on before the crowd could again block the street. Yet the words of the men stayed with him.

The Mongol charge of attempted thievery might be true. Or again, perhaps they only misunderstood the custom. Jalair did not know which. But instead of grumbling, the Mongols should see Shah Ala-u-Din, who would quickly set to right any wrong in Koresm, or correct their misunderstanding of what was really happening.

Surely, Jalair thought, there must be some honest explanation behind the actions of Khoresmian city governors. Jalair wished he could ask his old tutor, Sayyid Hussayn, about it.

Reaching Kaban's *yurt,* Jalair handed his reins to a servant, then went inside and took his place around the fire with the rest of the family.

They spoke little, each seeming to commit the scene to memory, for it would be many weeks before Kaban returned. Friends had come throughout the morning, but as the hour of departure neared, they left the family alone for its farewells.

Then Kaban leaned forward and put his hand on Dhuvik's shoulder. He spoke quietly, reminding his son of family duties, placing his trust in him.

How different was Kaban in the city from Kaban of the caravan trails! Jalair remembered that then Kaban's expression had been wary, his actions swift and powerful, his decisions made firmly and unsmilingly.

Perhaps Kaban, entering a strange country with strange languages and customs, felt he must be ready for anything. Jalair himself had felt this way when familiar Khoresm dropped below the western horizon and the land of Genghis Khan loomed before him. All the terrible stories people told of the Mongols had risen in his mind as the caravan entered the Takla Makan. Yet now Jalair lived and worked in the city of these terrible warriors, treated as a son by Kaban.

Then Kaban spoke to Jalair. "Work hard in your chosen task," he said. "And make me proud of you when I return."

"I will," Jalair promised. He was glad the plan he had formed that morning did not breach the hospitality of Kaban's family.

Then Kaban spoke gently to Chentai, bidding her farewell.

A roll of drums sounded outside, summoning the city to witness the sending off of the four richest caravans the world had ever seen.

"Now it is time to leave," said Kaban, rising. "Look for my return. Chentai, keep well the *yurt*. Sons, do your duties cheerfully."

Together they went outside. Servants had brought out and saddled three other horses, lining them up next to Jalair's mount.

Chentai tucked up her silken gown and mounted easily, and Jalair remembered her songs of the old days before the

coming of Genghis Khan, when tribe fought with tribe and the women rode beside their men carrying spare weapons in case their warrior-husbands should lose theirs in battle. It was no wonder other men called them Mongols, "the Brave People."

They trotted toward the arena where the caravans had been assembled. The crowd gave way before Kaban's family, for they all knew him well, and many called greetings and farewells.

They paused at the edge of the arena.

"Jalair," said Kaban. "I will spend some days in Samarkand. Is there anything I can do for you there?"

Jalair avoided his searching eyes. "No, nothing."

"Farewell, then." He twitched the reins and trotted to the head of his caravan, which would lead the others.

"If not the richest caravans, they are surely the most beautiful," laughed Chentai. Every animal had gay ribbons tied to its harness or around its neck. The carts and wagons had been brightly painted too, and every Mongol in the four caravans wore full battle armor. The armor would be taken off when they reached Khoresm, for they traveled as traders, not warriors.

Leaders, with the crests of their rank flowing from their helmets, galloped up and down the trains, making a last-minute inspection and shouting orders. Jalair was pleased to note that Kaban's caravan seemed to be the most orderly of them all.

In another caravan, two stubborn camels abruptly sat down and refused to move, though their tenders prodded them vigorously. The watching crowd started to laugh, and Jalair grinned as he remembered his own experiences with the ill-humored beasts of Urbano the Venetian.

Suddenly a great white horse paced out on the field.

"The Khan!" cried Dhuvik. "Do you not wish you had a horse like his, Jalair?"

"I would rather have one of his hawks."

The two camels were finally pulled up into position. The caravans waited in stiff, silent order, leaders at the heads of their trains. At a gesture of Genghis Khan, drummers began their roll. The standard-bearers, one to each caravan, lifted the great eagle-tipped poles, the nine white yak tails of the Khan fluttering in the breeze. Every horseman lifted his reins, and even the sleepy yaks seemed to hold their breaths waiting for the signal.

The roar of drums was snapped off by a crash of cymbals, and the four caravans began moving. Carts rumbled, horses trotted smartly, and camels loped along disdainfully. A long winding journey lay ahead, and at its end were Khoresm's great cities—Otrar, Urgendj, Meshed, Kabul.

Some boys on the edge of the crowd set off strings of firecrackers. Others ran behind the caravans, launching paper kites painted with hawks, dragons, warriors, or symbols of good luck. The creaks and rattles of the loaded wagons, the hoofbeats of yaks, camels, and horses were swallowed by the cheering of the crowd.

Dhuvik pulled on Chentai's silken sleeve as she gazed at the departing caravans. "Father will be home in a few weeks, Mother. Jalair and I will care for you until his return."

Chentai turned to them with a smile. "Then let us enjoy the remainder of the festival."

"Our class will begin drilling soon," Dhuvik said. "And after that the games start. Will you watch me win the lassoing contest?"

"I will miss both drill and contest," said Jalair. "Idikut awaits me in the mews. But I am entering the hawk trials later today, and you can see if I win." With a smile at Chentai, Jalair turned his horse away.

Trotting through the city was easier now, for almost everyone was at the arena. Even the entertainers and merchants were attracted to the crowd.

Jalair found Idikut in the mews talking earnestly with Chepe Noyon about the general's sakers. Chepe finally departed, confident of winning the prize for the best cast.

"We will be very busy in an hour or two, Jalair," said Idikut. "When the hawk meet begins, every warrior in Karakorum will swoop down at once and demand his hawks."

"I wish I could read these names," Jalair sighed, inspecting one of the wooden tags tied to the hawks' legs. On each was painted the name of the owner, but Jalair had not yet learned to decipher Mongol writing.

"Yatu is coming back to help us," Idikut replied. "While we have a moment's peace, help me gather the equipment for the trials."

Together they gathered bow perches and field cadges. "It is well we do not have to take care of the game, too," Jalair said, assembling the gear that would be packed in leather field kits. The Khan had sent out huntsmen to capture the quarry which would be released on the field during the hawking trials.

"We have work enough," Idikut agreed.

By the time the first warriors came for their hawks, the field equipment was packed and Yatu had arrived. At once he set to work, reading the owner's names on the wood tags and handing them their birds. While Idikut answered questions, gave advice, and mended broken flight feathers, Jalair was busy handing out jesses to replace those torn at the last moment, fastening bells, and helping some hawkers change ill-fitting hoods on their temperamental hawks. From time to time, Jalair would go over to Arrow at her place on one of the long bar perches. He stroked the peregrine encouragingly.

"Jalair, bring that goshawk tiercel at the end of the bottom perch," Yatu called to him.

Jalair unleashed the gos and brought him over, marveling at the sleek feathers and well-developed muscles. The hawk looked as if he were going to be a winner.

To Jalair's surprise, the gauntleted hand of a boy a little older than himself reached out to claim the goshawk. The boy expertly wrapped the leash around his fingers and left the mews. So calm and confident seemed the owner of the goshawk that Jalair began to worry about Arrow's chances.

And Arrow had to win.

At last it was time to go to the arena with the hawking gear. Jalair was to be in charge of the mews while Yatu and Idikut rode to the arena. "I will tell you when the boy's division begins," Yatu promised. It would be the last hawk contest of the day.

Since most of the hawkers had already claimed their birds, Jalair had little to do in the mews. He remembered to feed the birds still at hack, and to set out in the weathering yard hawks that had been inside for two days. Eagerly they stretched their wings and their talons gripped the wooden blocks. Some explored the ground as far as their leashes would let them.

Jalair toyed with the idea of going to the mews of the Golden Hawks and handling the famous birds his father had created. But he dismissed the notion. Yatu might chance to inspect the Goldens at that very moment.

Just then Yatu returned from the arena. "The boys' division will begin soon, Jalair."

Jalair started guiltily, as if Yatu could read his thoughts. He went to the perch and lifted Arrow gently to his fist. Then he went outside and mounted the way Idikut had taught him to when holding a hawk.

"I will stay a few moments to be certain all the boys have claimed their hawks," Yatu said. "Then I will go to the arena. Good luck with Arrow."

Jalair walked his horse, fearful of upsetting Arrow or causing a last-minute accident.

At the arena, he saw the gamekeepers at the far end, their cages set in rows. On the other side, hawks sat on the bow perches and cadges Idikut and Yatu had set up. A few cautious hawkers preferred keeping their birds on their fists, lest they become nervous from the excitement. Hawkers crowded around Idikut, discussing the performances of one another's birds. Chepe Noyon strutted proudly, rust-colored sakers side by side on his wrist. He looked as if his pair had won in the cast division.

Idikut saw Jalair and walked over. "The boys are just beginning. You will be the third to slip your hawk."

Jalair nodded and went to an empty bow perch, the sharpened ends of which had been pushed deeply into the earth. The top of the arch was padded, as were all of Idikut's perches. Jalair backed Arrow on the perch, then tied the leash to a ring.

"Jalair, I have been waiting for you," said Dhuvik from behind. He showed Jalair a large and beautifully lacquered Cathayan crossbow. "I won the lasso contest," he said proudly. "If Arrow wins, what will you ask for?"

"Wait and see," Jalair answered. "Look, there goes the first boy."

The first young hawker was the boy Jalair had noticed in the mews when he claimed his goshawk tiercel. The boy took his place with confidence before Genghis Khan's pavilion, and signaled to the gamekeepers.

Since goshawks do not wait on, the game was released first. The instant the hare jumped out of the cage, the boy pulled his tiercel into a prone position on his fist with the strap around its neck. Then drawing back his arm, he flung the goshawk into the air, slipping the leash free through the jess ring just in time to keep his hawk from hanging up.

The boy's arm was powerful, and the goshawk, catapulted from his wrist, easily gained hunting pitch.

Instantly the gos spotted the hare below. The tiercel stooped in a low angle, closing with the prey. Three times the gos abruptly changed direction as the hare dodged. Then his wings flared back and the feet came forward, claws open as he pounced and bound his quarry to the ground. It is in this manner that goshawks catch their prey, and the crowd

cheered the clean kill. Even Jalair had to admit the catch was well done.

"I hope Arrow can do as well," Jalair said uneasily.

"Are you really worried she will not win?" Dhuvik asked.

"I was hoping my knowledge of hawks would make up for lack of training time," said Jalair. "But the goshawk's master seems to have spent a good deal of time in the mews."

Dhuvik shaded his eyes against the sun. "I know him. He is the son of one of the Onan Valley generals."

The next hawk was a brancher gyrfalcon that had been flown before its feathers were fully formed. Its flight was ragged, and the final blow with closed fist lacked power. Before the gyr was called to fist, Jalair ran to Arrow's perch.

He slipped the leash and backed Arrow on his gauntleted fist. He remembered to walk slowly to his place before the

Khan's pavilion. It would never do to have Arrow hang up on her jesses just before the flight.

Jalair had not trained Arrow to the use of the neck strap used in catapulting hawks aloft. If the hawker became excited and didn't release the strap in time, the bird would be snapped to the ground, or worse, its neck would break. He unfastened Arrow's feather-tufted hood, and at the last moment, lifted it free of the falcon's head.

"Fly, Arrow!" he commanded sharply, at the same time giving his fist a quick toss upward. The peregrine took off without hesitation and planed upward, spiraling with slow powerful strokes of her tapered wings.

The black speckles of Arrow's white breast blurred with distance, and her bells grew fainter as she ringed to her pitch without a single wasted motion.

Jalair signaled the gamekeepers at the far end of the field. A grouse fluttered to freedom above the tall grass, then dropped to the ground, hidden from view.

Arrow dipped toward the ground, powerful wings adding speed to the stoop before they were folded back to her sleek blue and white body. Below, the grouse scented danger and exploded from the grassy field with a frantic blur of wings. But the bird was too slow, and the intelligent per had calculated well. Arrow never deviated an inch from her course as she plunged down over the quarry, striking out with closed fist.

Shouts of approval drowned out the tinkle of Arrow's bells as Jalair held out his fist to the returning falcon.

"A fine stoop, Jalair!" cried Idikut when Jalair returned to fasten Arrow to her bow perch.

"I have not yet won," Jalair cautioned.

"But you will," Dhuvik said.

"Not using a neck strap will put you over the Onan Valley general's son," Idikut declared. "And the other boys know little of hawking. They spend most of their time with horses and mock battles."

Idikut's words were true, for of the remaining young hawkers, only one had taken pains in training his bird. At that, he had over-lured, and his slim, fawn-colored lanner falcon was confused by the quarry's erratic dashes. For a moment it looked as if the lanner might rake away, but her master whistled encouragingly and the prey was finally taken.

There was a moment of quiet before the winner was announced.

And it was Jalair who was called before the Khan's pavilion, where the master of half the world sat with his generals. Yatu was among them, and Jalair was pleased he had taken the trouble to watch Arrow's fine performance.

"Well done, Jalair," said Genghis Khan as the boy bowed low before him. "It is the custom for the winner to name his prize. Yet I ask you to allow me to select it, for I have prepared a gift more fitting than any you could name."

The Khan's words could not be lightly brushed aside. Jalair was silent as he faced this dilemma. He knew not what Genghis Khan planned for him, but he did know that the richest gift in the world was nothing beside his own choice. He thought out his reply carefully.

"O Khan, the reason I tried so hard to win this contest was to have the privilege of asking for the one thing that means most to me in the world." He stopped, wondering if he had insulted this conqueror of nations.

Just the faintest flicker of displeasure crossed the Khan's bearded face, and then the smile returned. "Then let it be. What is it that you prize so highly?"

"I would like nothing more," Jalair said in a rush lest he lose his nerve, "than a pair of Golden Hawks."

There was a sudden silence around the pavilion, as from indrawn breaths. Astonishment flashed on the faces of the officers and nearby guards.

The Khan's eyes changed.

He was no longer smiling.

10 Talons for Revenge

In a rush of whispers, Jalair's bold request flashed through the crowd, silencing their jovial talk. Jalair felt all eyes fastened upon him, and suddenly he wished he had not dared ask for the Golden Hawks.

Yatu stepped forward, and the clank of his armor rang clearly in the silence. The warrior gave a short, military bow to Genghis Khan. "If it please you, my Khan," he said, "allow me to explain to Jalair." He turned to the boy. "No one may own or hunt with the Golden Hawks except the Khan himself. The hawks were presented to him some years ago, and no more fitting honor than this could be presented to the mightiest warrior in the world, the Khan of Khans."

"I—I did not know," Jalair faltered.

Genghis Khan's grimness died as Yatu spoke, and now he said gently, "The boy does not yet know all our customs, Yatu." He turned to Jalair. "I know it grieves a young hawker's heart to see the Golden Hawks kept in their mews instead of being slipped to game. Yet it is in this manner that I return the honor the giver of the hawks has done me. Some day the Golden Hawks will be flown in hunting—"

"—when Torgul returns," Yatu finished.

"Let us speak no more of this incident," the Khan said. "Jalair, will you name another prize?"

"Only that which you would give me, O Khan," replied Jalair, at once relieved and disappointed.

A guard stepped up with a folded cloth in his arms. The Khan took it from him and shook it open. It was a blue cloak, lined with white silk, and on the back was embroidered a silver gyrfalcon on wing. It was the cloak of the Khan's Hawker, exactly like Idikut's, but made for Jalair.

With his own hands, Genghis Khan placed the Hawker's cloak on Jalair, fastening the silver chain around the boy's neck. "You well have earned this mark of the Khan's Hawker," the Khan said.

Only that morning Jalair had longed for such an insignia of his profession. Now with the cloak hanging from his shoulders, he remembered its deeper significance. He wanted to rip it off and hurl it at Genghis Khan's feet. Yet he had the wit to bow low and thank the Khan for his gift.

More than a cloak had been given him. By this action the Khan had raised Jalair to a member of his court. It was an honor not to be borne lightly, for now Jalair was trapped into a loyalty he did not honestly feel.

Yet there had been no way to refuse.

The days following the festival were uneventful ones. Jalair wore the Hawker's cloak with pride, mingled with shame that Darien's son should be honored by his father's enemies. Dhuvik continued his studies at the officers' school, eagerly recounting the drill with weapons, and then grumbling at the scholars who drilled the cadets with the pen instead of the sword.

Jalair and Idikut spent long lazy days, either in the mews or racing beneath the hawks they exercised. Twice they went hunting by themselves, and Arrow proved that her victory on the festival day was no accident.

Yet Jalair fretted over the Golden Hawks. He had been so sure he would own a pair after Arrow won the contest. He had dreamed of holding on his fist and sending into the sky Darien's hawks, Jalair's own hawks by right. It was bitter to have come so close and then be denied. And the longing for the Golden Hawks grew greater and greater until flying even Arrow seemed poor sport.

He wondered, as he worked beside Idikut, what Genghis Khan would think of his honored Torgul if he knew the Golden Hawks had been given him by a murderer. For if Torgul had been in a position to give the Golden Hawks to the Khan, then how could Jalair any longer doubt that it was he who had stolen them? Jalair knew by now that Mongols adhered to a strict code of laws, called the *Yassa*. Much of the code came from tribal tradition, but Genghis Khan was the first to have them set in writing. A deed such as Torgul's would be punished.

Still, Jalair knew not what lie Torgul might have told, and because of this he feared to reveal himself as Darien's son.

Yet the Golden Hawks were but three bow-shots away

from the mews where Jalair worked. Nor could Jalair forever ignore the gold specks glittering in the morning sun as Yatu exercised them on the plains. And so his heart ached to fly the Golden Hawks, until there was only one thing to do.

He saw his chance when one night Dhuvik announced that once again his class was going on maneuvers in the foothills. It would take all afternoon, and Yatu as usual would supervise the mock battle.

The next morning passed as usual in the mews. In the afternoon, Jalair asked if he could go into the mountains. "I want to see if I can catch some branchers by myself," he said.

"You have not yet mastered the climbing of cliffs," Idikut said. "But you may try your luck. Be careful not to fall."

Jalair gathered together the nets, traps, and other equipment he would use, and outside he fastened them to his saddle. Then he trotted through the city, slowing to a walk when he came near the mews of the Golden Hawks.

There was no one around, and even if someone did see Jalair trot off with a pair of Goldens, nothing would be said. Did not Jalair wear the cloak of the Khan's Hawker?

Jalair stepped into the mews, and stopped a moment to let his eyes become accustomed to the gloom. Then breathlessly he approached the beautiful hawks. Bells tinkled as they shifted their feet, sensing the presence of a stranger. Jalair would have liked to examine all of Darien's hawks, yet he must allow time to bring back a few branchers from the mountains to show Idikut, and he was determined to fly the Goldens in a hidden mountain valley he knew from past trappings. Quickly, he began untying the leash of the nearest Golden.

"Well, Jalair," said Yatu.

Jalair whirled, his heart pounding.

Yatu stood before the doorway to the breeding room, where he must have been working since Jalair entered the mews. Too late, Jalair remembered that Yatu returned frequently to inspect the Goldens. Now the scarred warrior waited for Jalair's explanation, and the boy was conscious of Yatu's strength.

"I—I wanted to be sure the hawks were all right," Jalair said. He tried hard to look straight into Yatu's eyes so that the warrior would believe him. "Dhuvik said you would be away for the afternoon, and I thought they might need care."

"The hawks are fed and watered, and I exercised them this morning," Yatu answered. "And as you see, I return frequently to attend to them." He approached and took the loosened leash from Jalair's hands.

"I was just tying this on," Jalair said, watching Yatu's large strong hands fasten the leash to the perch. "Sometimes restless hawks loosen them."

"Yes," Yatu said. "Sometimes the hawks slip their leashes if the leather is old and worn."

"Or if the leather is stiff with newness," Jalair countered, knowing well the leash had not been old.

"And if a hawker does not know his knots well." Yatu grinned, quickly forming an expert tie.

"I must go now," Jalair said, edging toward the doorway.

"Jalair."

The quiet firmness of Yatu's voice held him as imprisoned as if he were bound hand and foot. The caretaker of the Golden Hawks stepped close to him. "The boys I help instruct in warfare are hard workers and learn their lessons well," Yatu said. "They are impatient for the day they may lead a charge into battle. Yet they must study and practice for years until they have earned that privilege. So it is with young hawkers."

Not knowing how to answer, Jalair waited in silence.

"Idikut says you do your work well, that you have the heart and hand of a true hawker," Yatu continued. "Yet, as with the cadet officers, you also have years of training ahead before you can have complete charge of a hawk mews. Work hard and willingly, Jalair, and who knows? Perhaps some day you will have charge of the Golden Hawks, if Torgul does not return."

The words rushed out before Jalair could silence his thoughts. "Who is Torgul and where has he gone?"

Yatu's eyes narrowed. "Do not trouble yourself with

what is not your concern. Idikut will be looking for you, Jalair."

Jalair left quickly, lest Yatu think of more to say. He swung into the saddle and trotted out of the city, through the surrounding plains to the rim of mountains beyond.

He hunted half-heartedly for young hawks, hardly caring if his bow-nets were set properly. Three hours of brooding effort netted him four branchers. One was of such poor quality that he released it. The others were put into falcon socks which fitted snugly around their bodies but allowed the head and feet to protrude. This prevented them from beating their wings and damaging their flight feathers. Then Jalair placed them in compartments of his wicker basket and started back.

The round humps of *yurts* and squares of *kibitkas* and camel carts stretched their purple shadows over the plain as Jalair rode back to the mews with the three undistinguished hawks.

"Never mind, Jalair," Idikut consoled him, noticing his unhappy expression. "This was your first hunting trip alone. Soon you will bring in more and better hawks."

Jalair hooded one of the branchers and began slipping off the falcon sock, but Idikut took the hawk from him.

"It is evening, and you have done a full day's work," the Hawk Master told him.

Jalair bade him good night, and left quietly, half expecting Idikut to call him back. But apparently Yatu had not spoken to the Hawk Master, for Idikut was busy with the branchers when Jalair departed.

For the next few days, Jalair worked very well indeed. He came earlier in the morning, and by the time Idikut arrived, the mews had been cleaned, the hawks watered, and all equipment made ready for the day's work. Yet not once by word or sign did the Hawk Master show whether or not Yatu had told of catching Jalair in the mews of the Golden Hawks.

From time to time, Yatu visited Idikut to discuss matters of hawking. Then Jalair found work to keep him out of the way of the scarred warrior, though the keeper of the Goldens seemed friendly enough toward him.

One night when Jalair returned to Kaban's *yurt*, he found Dhuvik waiting impatiently.

"If you are that hungry," Jalair laughed, sitting near the fire, "then begin eating without me."

Dhuvik poured himself a horn of milk from the leather sack a servant handed him. The boys were eating alone tonight, for Chentai was visiting friends. "Not hunger but news makes me wait for you," Dhuvik said, cutting a joint from the roast near the fire. "You hawkers are so buried in the mews you never hear of what happens in the world."

Jalair took his bowl of rice from the servant. "And what news is there?"

"A prisoner has been brought in today," Dhuvik said. "He is a Khoresmian named Iskander. They say he is from the court of Shah Ala-u-Din."

From the court of the Shah!

Jalair nearly dropped his bowl of rice. "Is—" He could hardly bring himself to ask. "Is there war?"

Dhuvik looked startled. "Oh, no! War would destroy our trade with Koresm. It is only that this Iskander is a scoundrel seeking favor with Genghis Khan."

"Then how was he captured?"

"It is said he came up to one of our post stations near the Khoresm border. He demanded to be taken to the Khan, and so he was. He arrived only this morning, and was at once eager to tell freely of the Shah's army, location of forts, and to describe new weapons. This for a price."

"The Khoresmian was a traitor?" Jalair could hardly believe his ears.

Dhuvik laughed. "More merchant than traitor, perhaps. For Iskander said he would not say a word until he counted gold in his hand. Of course, the Khan was angry."

"Because Iskander's price was too high?"

"No!" Dhuvik exclaimed. "Never once in his reign has Genghis Khan used the services of traitors! He was angry that this man would dare insult him in this fashion."

Jalair was greatly surprised. Treacherous men selling information to other governments were not uncommon, though to think of a Khoresmian doing such a thing was bitter indeed. "What will happen to Iskander?" Jalair had entirely forgotten the evening meal.

"He will be sent back to the Shah on the next caravan to Urgendj," Dhuvik said, reaching for a handful of dried fruit and nuts. "Let Shah Ala-u-Din punish his own traitors."

"That is a noble act," Jalair said a little skeptically. "Then the Khan expects nothing for his trouble?"

Dhuvik laughed again. "Ordinarily he sends traitors home and asks for nothing in return. But this is a good chance to free our caravans from the greedy demands of Khoresm city governors, and this is the bargain the Khan will make with Shah Ala-u-Din."

Suddenly Jalair saw through the Khan's public explanation of Iskander's imprisonment. No traitor was Iskander, but a hostage, kidnapped to force a bargain with Khoresm's Shah.

Jalair thought the Khan's action hasty and ill-advised. Willing as Shah Ala-u-Din would be to straighten out any misunderstanding, Jalair knew the Khoresmian ruler would never allow the Mongols to force him into any decision, just or otherwise. To bow to Mongol demands would cause the Shah's army to lose faith in him, and perhaps to revolt.

"What is being done with Iskander while the Khan waits for the next westward caravan?" Jalair asked.

"He was placed in a *kang*, and put in a prison *yurt* that is well guarded." At Jalair's puzzled look, Dhuvik explained. "A *kang* is a heavy wooden slab, split in two and hinged at one end. There are holes which hold the neck and wrists when the *kang* is placed on a man's shoulders. The other end is fastened securely. Thus, even if a prisoner should manage to escape, he cannot use his hands and so is easily recaptured." Then Dhuvik began telling of what happened during the school day.

News of the prisoner from Khoresm spread rapidly, it seemed, for when Jalair went to the mews the following morning, Idikut mentioned it, though usually the Hawk Master took little note of anything but hawking.

Jalair paused in his work, trying to sound casual. "I don't think I ever saw the prison *yurt*. Where is it?"

"On the other side of the market place, near the river," Idikut replied, his hands skillfully fashioning new leather hoods for the hawks. "If you care to see it, you will know it by its black color and the two guards at the entrance."

Jalair passed near the market place on the way home every night. He could easily contrive to ride past the prison *yurt*. Perhaps he could find some excuse for seeing the prisoner, though he must be careful not to bring suspicion upon himself.

He started to carry the weathering blocks out to the yard enclosure, but Idikut stopped him. "Not today, Jalair. The older hawks are restless, and we will take them out on the plains to stretch their wings."

Together they packed field kits, and tied the older hawks to two field cadges. By now, Jalair was skilled enough to be trusted with carrying a cadge on horseback, though tied to his were the less valuable hawks, including his own Arrow.

The skies were high and clear, and the long grass on the plains was swept by a cold fresh wind, a sign that the short steppe summer was drawing to a close. It was indeed, as Idikut said, "hawking weather."

A long hail from behind made them pull their horses to a walk, and they waited for Yatu to trot up. He held before him on the saddle a field cadge with three Golden Hawks—two falcons and a tiercel. Jalair tore his eyes from the brilliant birds so the men could not see his longing for them.

"Will you lay a wager, Idikut, that the Goldens outfly your hawks?" Yatu grinned as they continued across the plains together.

"No," Idikut answered. "Though mine are better trained, even an ill-managed Golden far outflies the finest of trained peregrines."

Yatu laughed, and the three rode on until the city was low on the horizon behind them and the mountains still rose far ahead. Idikut stood in his stirrups and examined the plains carefully. "Good," he approved, dismounting with his cadge. "The herds are on the east and south of the city, away from us. Will you fly the Goldens first, Yatu?"

"Loose your hawks first," the warrior answered, carefully

setting his cadge of Goldens on the ground. "Then I will show you what flying is!"

Jalair picketed all three horses, then went to help Idikut. He could hardly wait to see the Goldens in flight. How shoddy even Arrow looked beside them! It seemed to take forever to untie each hawk, hand it to Idikut, see it flung into the air and wait impatiently until it was called to the fist.

At last it was Arrow's turn in the skies, and Jalair slipped the peregrine himself. The falcon's graceful circles failed to thrill him this time, for he was thinking of the Golden Hawks. Though he knew now that no one but the Khan could hope to own them, and only Yatu was allowed to care for them, he still hoped he might have the privilege of slipping a Golden Hawk into the sky. Jalair was bursting to ask the favor.

Yet when Arrow returned to his fist, the memory of Yatu's accusing eyes in the mews of the Goldens stayed his tongue. Jalair pretended indifference as Yatu prepared to slip the Golden Hawks.

"You will see three golden hunters in the sky at once," Yatu promised. He placed one of the falcons on his fist, slipped off the hood and flung the hawk into the sky. Working quickly but carefully, Yatu sent the tiercel up. Then he put the second falcon on his fist and unhooded her.

Jalair pretended to be absorbed with quieting the still unhooded Arrow as the falcon shifted restlessly on his gauntleted hand.

Up, up flashed the twin streaks of feathered gold!

Jalair could ignore them no longer. He held his breath as he followed the two priceless spirals of gold that seemed to form as falcon and tiercel ringed up, their bells tinkling fainter with each wing-stroke.

Even Yatu, arrested in the act of slipping the third Golden Hawk, gazed in fascination, the unhooded falcon still on his fist.

Silently, the three watched the hawks as they reached their pitch and waited on, each turning and turning on one pointed wing. The sunlight winked with every turn of their bodies.

Jalair swallowed hard as he studied the flashing gold. Darien, his father, had himself created this magnificent breed of hawk.

Then Jalair's blood ran cold, for Yatu was speaking.

"Ah, how Darien would love to see them wheel in the sky!" the warrior exulted, all but forgetting the unhooded Golden falcon still on his wrist. "Perhaps even now Darien's spirit watches the flight of the Goldens from behind the Gate of Heaven."

Rage stormed through Jalair's mind as he heard his father's name spoken in mockery. Vengefully Jalair jerked his wrist, dropping one end of Arrow's leash. He felt the leather slip through the jess ring, and the spring of the startled peregrine from his hand. Directly ahead of the falcon was an obstruction, Yatu's face, and Arrow instinctively brought up her talons to strike.

With scarcely time for a muttered cry, Yatu flung up his arm, dropping the leash. With a bound, the Golden on his fist shot off to meet the threat.

The two hawks plunged together, claws foremost. The frantic beating of their wings fanned the air. Feathers flew from the fighting hawks as the Golden's heavier weight forced both to the ground, bound together. The Golden landed uppermost, fought free, then drove again toward Arrow on the ground.

The Golden falcon fluttered away from her prey, and began preening until Yatu's voice brought her to his fist. The peregrine lay still upon the ground.

It happened within a few seconds, yet anger and fear stretched out that moment for Jalair until he thought he could neither move nor speak again.

The look of horror on Idikut's face drained away when he saw Yatu was unmarked. Wonderingly, the Hawk Master turned to Jalair. "What happened, Jalair?"

"The—the leash slipped," Jalair muttered, surprised he could use his voice after all. When only silence answered him, he went on, "I was watching the Goldens, and I forgot about Arrow's being on my fist. I guess I let the leash go."

Relief flooded Idikut's features, and he said gruffly, "Well, there is no harm done, but you must be more careful if you would be trusted with hawks. Return to the mews. I will bring back both cadges myself."

As Jalair turned away from the men, he saw Yatu's face. The warrior's eyes were cold. He knew Arrow had been purposely loosed.

Jalair felt his legs go weak as he walked back to his horse. A spot in the middle of his back seemed to burn as he half expected a blow from a sword. He turned his mount toward the city, and sat very straight as he trotted back, stifling the urge to gallop.

The mews seemed almost deserted with Idikut and the best hawks away. Jalair busied himself with routine work, trying hard not to think of what had happened on the plain. Yet every time he passed Arrow's place on one of the long perches, his heart ached.

He thought of the Golden Hawks that were rightfully his, and yet not his. He thought of Yatu, who had mockingly spoken of Darien's death, and his heart turned to a cold hard lump.

There was no real reason to look upon Yatu as companion to Darien's slayer. Certainly Torgul had lied to Genghis Khan when he presented him with the Golden Hawks, and Yatu would believe the same lie.

But to hear Darien's name spoken by a Mongol had fired the same urge to avenge his father as had lifted Jalair's hand against Kaban in Samarkand's market place so long ago.

Anger had sustained him on the plain even before those accusing eyes, but now in the silence of the mews, fear took its place. Had Yatu guessed Jalair was Darien's son?

Jalair kept busy, but when the work was at an end and Idikut had not yet returned, he decided to leave, though the day was but half gone. Perhaps Yatu's wrath and Idikut's grimness would be lessened tomorrow.

As he trotted away from the mews, Jalair remembered the prison *yurt*. He turned toward the market place, and near the river that flowed through its center, he found the black *yurt* with two heavily armed guards standing before the closed doorway. No smoke rose from the *yurt* in spite of the noon hour. Jalair wondered if they were feeding the man called Iskander.

He lingered near the *yurt*, dismounting and pretending to adjust the girth. He heard one of the guards call out to a passing merchant. The merchant, an Arab, crossed the street to the prison *yurt* and stood talking to the guard.

"He has been calling out all day," the guard complained. "I know not what tongue he uses. Can you understand what the prisoner wants?"

"Does he speak Arabic?" the merchant asked.

Jalair quickly led his horse over to the guards.

"I don't know," the guard was telling the Arab.

"I speak the tongue of the Khoresmians," Jalair said. "I can translate for you."

"Then go in," said the guard, pulling aside the heavy felt curtain for Jalair. "And if he is doing nothing but complaining, tell him to be silent."

It was dark and stifling inside the prison *yurt*. The smoke hole was closed.

"Is there at last one to heed my cries in this terrible country?" cried an anguished voice in Turki.

"Where are you?" Jalair asked in the same tongue.

From the dark came a hollow desperate laugh. "You mock me. I am here. Where else?"

"Let me get used to the dark," Jalair answered.

Gradually he was able to see a little. Dim light filtered through the heavy dark cloth, and Jalair realized that the prison *yurt* was black to prevent signals being passed. At last Jalair made out the man's shape.

The captive hunched on the ground, his wrists held level with his shoulders by a heavy board that locked hands and neck between its two halves. This was the *kang* of which Dhuvik had spoken.

"Is it true you are from the court of Shah Ala-u-Din?" Jalair asked.

"True enough," Iskander replied, "though I am not likely to see it again."

Jalair felt around the dirt floor of the darkened *yurt*. "Is there no lamp here?"

"Yes, it is lighted when they bring me what they choose to call food," Iskander growled.

At last Jalair found the small sheep-fat lamp. He reached

into his jacket for the Cathayan fire-striker one of his new friends had given him when he arrived in Karakorum. After four tries, he managed to light the wick.

Jalair lifted the lamp, holding it out. The sputtering flame fell on the disheveled hair and angry eyes of Iskander.

Jalair gasped. The lamp, falling from his numb fingers, struck the earthen floor and went out.

But even in the darkness, Jalair's mind still beheld the features of the man in the *kang*. They had met before, in Kurush's garden.

Iskander was the man who had come to take Jalair to Urgendj.

11 The Shadow of the Kang

The prison *yurt* plunged into a silence as dense as its darkness. Jalair recovered his senses and fumbled for the lamp. He lighted it again, and set it on the floor between himself and Iskander.

Now it was the captive's turn to be surprised, for so briefly did the lamp flare the first time that he had not then recognized the boy from the house of Kurush.

"You are Jalair," he said, his eyes shining. "You ran away from Samarkand rather than be sent to Urgendj."

"I did not run away," Jalair protested. "I came after the Golden Hawks." Unconsciously he whispered, but now he realized no one could understand their conversation since both spoke in Turki. "I wanted to bring a pair back to the Shah so he would let me become a hawker instead of a gentleman."

"Bring back the Golden Hawks?" Iskander stared at Jalair unbelievingly.

"I can do it," Jalair insisted. "I know where they are kept. I have seen them flown." Back rushed the picture of Arrow driving toward Yatu. Jalair shut it out. "I know the Shah would grant me anything I asked if he got the Goldens, because my father bred them in his honor."

"Yes, yes." Iskander nodded as vigorously as the *kang* allowed. "A fine plan, Jalair, but foolish for a boy of your years. That is why I came seeking you."

"You knew I traveled to Karakorum?" Jalair asked in surprise.

"Not at once," Iskander said, "or word would have been sent to the frontier guards to bring you back. It was some days later that Kurush remembered you often spoke of the Golden Hawks. We knew then you had set out for the land of Genghis Khan. Yet you are a boy, and the Shah had made you my responsibility. I could not let you go to be killed by those who slew your father, enslaved your mother, and stole the Golden Hawks. I followed as swiftly as possible, searching for you."

"Your journey was a needless one," Jalair explained. "The

Mongols know not I am Darien's son, and I am in no danger." Yet the vision of Yatu's cold eyes was clear.

"Since Khoresm and Genghis Khan's empire are at peace," Iskander continued, "I saw no reason to disguise myself, and thought even to receive generous treatment from the Mongols because of my office. Oh, those treacherous cowards! No sooner was I beyond Khoresm's frontiers than they turned upon me. I was bound up like a criminal and sent post haste to their Khan."

"They say you demanded to be taken to the Khan," Jalair told him.

"Ah, so they lie even among themselves!" Iskander exclaimed. "When I was brought to Genghis Khan, he found scholars who knew Arabic. For hours I was questioned on court secrets, the Shah's army, and asked to name those who I thought might turn traitor for gold. Of course, there were no names to give, for what Khoresmian would betray Shah Ala-u-Din?"

"That is true," Jalair sighed with relief. Though he was certain the story of Iskander's supposed treachery was false, he was glad for reassurance.

"I was afraid to ask about you," Iskander went on, shifting the weight of the heavy *kang* on his shoulders. "Already I feared you were a prisoner, and might come to further harm if they found I knew you."

"I have the freedom of the city," Jalair said. He was about to add with pride that he was assistant to the Khan's Hawk Master, but he was aware of a sudden fear that Iskander might think he had turned his back on his native Khoresm. "They think I have come to live among them," Jalair explained.

"When Genghis Khan found I would not betray Shah Ala-u-Din," Iskander continued, "he had me placed in this wooden collar and shut up here. Every hour, one of the guards enters to question me again. But with all my heart, I resist their bribes and threats."

"I am sorry your concern for me put you in such danger," Jalair said sincerely. "Yet they say the Khan will soon send you back to Khoresm in return for privileges in trading."

"He lies!" Iskander snarled. "He wishes his barbarians to think him an honorable man. When the Khan grows impatient with my loyalty to the Shah, I will be slain. Then he will invent some excuse for his people so they will say he acted justly."

"Is this true?" Jalair cried out. "The Mongols have been grumbling that they are asked to give gifts to Khoresmian city governors. Surely they will let you live in return for the Shah's promise that they need not do so."

Iskander's dark eyes glowed in the lamp flames. "A poor excuse for keeping me alive until they force me into betrayal! Every caravan freely gives to city governors. There is no reason why the arrogant Mongols should be angered by this old custom. And if it does anger them, they need not send caravans to Khoresm at all. No, it is not trade privilege, but the Shah's secrets they are after." Iskander licked his dry lips and his eyes roamed around the *yurt*.

Jalair hunted in the gloom until he found a leather bottle of water, and he gave a drink to the captive.

"Jalair," Iskander said in a low ominous tone, "I have heard the Khan himself threaten me with death. I have only a few days before he grows weary of my stubbornness."

Jalair wished fervently that Iskander had not followed him to Karakorum. Yet in a way, it was his fault that the Shah's courtier now languished in a prison *yurt*. "I will rescue you," Jalair promised, though he had not the faintest idea how to bring this about.

The prisoner's eyes lit up with hope, then dulled with despair. "How can a mere boy outwit the Khan's army?"

"They trust me here," Jalair assured him. Remembering Arrow's death on the plains that morning, he wondered how long that trust would endure. "I found my way over mountains and through deserts, and I am sure I can think of a way to free you." Yet it was Kaban's protection that had seen him through the long journey. Jalair brushed the thought away angrily.

"It must be done quickly," Iskander said.

Jalair thought for a moment. "The Khan is trying to deceive his people into thinking that he is a just man. He said he would send you away on the next westward caravan."

"He will kill me instead," Iskander declared.

"But not until the next caravan goes out," Jalair pointed out. "I will hear of such a caravan, and I have until then to think of a way to rescue you."

"You will come also, will you not?" Iskander asked.

Jalair shook his head. "I am not going back to Khoresm until I can take a pair of Golden Hawks with me. But the most important thing now is your return to Urgendj."

Jalair snuffed out the lamp and rose to go. "What excuse shall I give the guards for our long talk? They say you were calling out to them."

"Say only I wished for water. As for our talk, tell them I pleaded with you to ask the Khan to free me. And Jalair, pretend scorn for my request, or you shall find yourself in a *kang*, too."

Jalair nodded, even though Iskander could not see him. He thrust aside the curtain and stepped through the low doorway, blinking in the bright sunlight.

"What did the scoundrel wish?" one of the guards asked him in Mongol.

"Only for water," Jalair answered. He added the excuse Iskander had invented, then mounted and trotted homeward.

The *yurt* was empty, except for the servants, for Jalair had left the mews at midday. He spent the afternoon polishing his boots and harness, all the while thinking of Iskander.

How could he, Jalair, whisk a prisoner out from under Genghis Khan's eagle eyes when he could not even lay hands on a pair of Golden Hawks?

"In the old days, there was war enough to keep the army ready for action," said Dhuvik. "But during these peaceful years, the warriors grow unwary from lack of unexpected raids. That is why everyone is certain the Khan is preparing surprise maneuvers for the entire army."

"But if everyone knows of these plans, how can the warriors be surprised?" Jalair wanted to know.

Dhuvik grinned. "Where will the 'enemy forces' strike? Which of the troops has the Khan set aside for each side? Only the commanders know, and they will not tell until the mock raids begin." He sighed longingly. "I hope the cadet officers are allowed to join the maneuvers."

This explained the exhausted messengers who had ridden into Karakorum on foam-flecked horses that day.

Jalair had seen the first arrive while on his way to the mews that morning. For the past two days, he had risen earlier and had done extra work in the hope that Idikut would not speak to him of Yatu's narrow escape from Arrow's talons. And as yet, Idikut had said nothing of the incident.

On this morning, Karakorum had not yet stirred, and a cold dawn lay upon the Khan's city.

A pounding of hoofs echoed through the clear air, and turning in his saddle, Jalair saw a distant horseman relentlessly driving his mount. Sunlight flashed on the copper tiger tablet the rider wore on his chest, and from this Jalair knew him to be a post rider. He had seen them gallop into the city before, but never in such lathered haste.

The messenger drew nearer, and was soon lost behind the round humps of the *yurts*, though the hoofs rang sharply on the hard-packed dirt streets.

Jalair continued his way to the mews, and as usual for the last two days, had most of the work finished by the time Idikut arrived. For the third morning, the Hawk Master failed to remind Jalair of the incident on the plains.

It was when Idikut sent him to the market place to buy leather that Jalair saw the second post rider gallop in, wearily hunched over in his saddle, his horse laboring.

"What news?" asked the leather merchant after Jalair made his purchase.

"I know not," Jalair answered, himself wondering.

"Perhaps the Khan will make an announcement today," the merchant said, curious for the news that sent two exhausted messengers to Genghis Khan.

Jalair told Idikut of the messengers, but the Hawk Master only shrugged. As usual, he took little heed of anything beyond the mews.

The afternoon passed quietly as both worked. Perhaps Yatu had said nothing of catching Jalair unleashing a Golden Hawk, or of his suspicions that Jalair had deliberately tossed

Arrow into his face. And Idikut seemed to believe Arrow's release was indeed accidental. Jalair began to turn his attention to finding some way to bring about Iskander's freedom.

That evening, as he rode home, Jalair noticed that every warrior in Karakorum seemed to be attracted toward the great white *yurt* of Genghis Khan in the center of the city.

It was Dhuvik who gave an explanation for the day's unusual activity. "All the boys in the officers' school are talking about maneuvers," he said. "The officers who instruct us—Chepe Noyon, Yatu, Soo and the others—were called to a council in the Khan's *yurt*. We had to spend the day with the scholars who thought it a fine time to have us practice writing."

"It seems to me the cadet officers are too inexperienced to take part in real army maneuvers," Jalair said.

"Last year the whole school took part," Dhuvik told him. "That day all the classes were drilling on the plains when an 'enemy' force swooped down on them. Only a few cadets were taken captive. Genghis Khan allowed the students who escaped to join the other side and act as scouts for the rest of the maneuvers. This year, the Khan will surely allow us first year cadets at least to stand guard."

The next morning, as Jalair rode to his work, he noticed that every warrior seemed busy. Those who formerly spent their time standing guard, wrestling, horse racing, and matching stories of war heros, were now fashioning arrows, making slings and lassos, repairing harness, and sharpening swords.

Idikut was already at the mews when Jalair arrived. "We are to care for the Golden Hawks," Idikut said. "Yatu is in council with the Khan and the other officers, and so has no time for the birds." The Hawk Master seemed to have something on his mind, for he spoke little to Jalair while they fed, watered, and exercised their hawks.

It was when they went to the mews of the Golden Hawks that Idikut spoke his thoughts. First he set Jalair to routine tasks, not letting him handle any of the Goldens.

"Jalair," began Idikut carefully, "a hawker's work requires much patience and obedience to orders. You have done well

the weeks you have been in Karakorum, and you must not let ambition or—or envy, ruin your good position."

Jalair felt the rush of blood to his cheeks, and he bent over his work, unable to face the Hawk Master.

"You are fortunate that Kaban spoke for you to the Khan," Idikut went on. "And luckier still that the Khan at once made you an apprentice hawker. You have earned the cloak of the Khan's Hawker. Someday you will have complete charge of a mews, if—" Idikut paused for emphasis, "if you follow every order given you."

To Jalair's relief, Idikut did not continue, but went back to his work. He was glad too, that though Yatu had apparently told Idikut about catching Jalair in the Goldens' mews, the Hawk Master did not read a deeper meaning into the action.

"It is true I envied," Jalair said. "And I am sorry these feelings made me do things I should not have. It will never happen again." And Jalair resolved to stay away from the Golden Hawks and their keeper as much as possible.

"Well, it is forgotten," said Idikut.

The rest of the day passed as usual, though Jalair was still not permitted to handle the Goldens himself. Idikut seemed content with Jalair's apology, but Darien's son was certain that Yatu harbored a deep grudge against him. The scarred warrior would need little excuse to take his revenge.

Jalair was angry with himself for having been caught unleashing the Golden. He should not have slipped Arrow either, though the mockery with which Darien's name was spoken had momentarily banished his reasoning.

He saw now that he had tried too soon to avenge the wrong done his father. A boy was no match against seasoned warriors. Plainly, a new plan would have to be worked out, perhaps one that would take years of earning Mongol respect while he walked the tightrope of Yatu's lurking vengeance.

Meanwhile, Iskander was a problem calling for immediate action. Jalair would have his best chance when the army left Karakorum to go on maneuvers.

Late that afternoon, the quiet of the mews was invaded by a distant cry as a courier rode through the city. From time to time came the notes of a horn, followed by the reading of the proclamation.

Though he could not hear the actual words, Jalair was surprised that the maneuvers would begin so soon. Dhuvik had told him it took many weeks to gather the Khan's great army from the reaches of the empire, and to prepare for marching.

The courier's announcements had ceased when Jalair rode home that evening, though the streets were crowded with people excitedly discussing the proclamation.

Dhuvik ran out of the *yurt* shouting, "Have you heard the news?"

"Are you to go with the army on maneuvers?" Jalair asked, smiling at Dhuvik's breathless excitement.

"Maneuvers indeed!" Dhuvik exclaimed. "Then you have not heard what happened at Otrar?"

Instantly Jalair was alert. Otrar was a Khoresmian city situated on the eastern border, north of the Tien Shan. Its outskirts touched hands with Genghis Khan's empire.

"You know that during the trade festival four of the richest caravans ever seen set out for Khoresm," Dhuvik said rapidly as Jalair nodded. "When the caravan sent to Otrar reached that city, Governor Inaldjuk seized it for his own."

"Inaldjuk seized the caravan?" cried Jalair, hardly believing his ears. "What will the Khan do?"

"Genghis Khan," Dhuvik told him, "has declared war on Khoresm."

A war against Shah Ala-u-Din!

Jalair's throat went dry, for he was a Khoresmian. Iskander must be rescued without delay, and he himself must flee.

He must flee before Genghis Khan placed him in a *kang* too.

12 Escape from Karakorum

"They say Inaldjuk's eyes grew large with greed when he saw the gifts our caravan leader presented to him," stated the warrior.

The other soldiers seated around the fire outside their host's *yurt* nodded in agreement.

"Was it then he threw our men into prison?" Dhuvik asked.

Though dusk had not yet fallen, Karakorum was reddened with firelight. It seemed as if every household had moved its cooking fire outside, so everyone could discuss the incident at Otrar with friends and neighbors. Not since the trade festival had Jalair seen the city swarming with such activity, yet this new excitement had an air of grimness that frightened him.

Chentai had told her son she would eat the evening meal with friends. Servants prepared food for Dhuvik and Jalair, but, moved by the restless spirit of the city, the boys had left the meal untouched to wander through the streets. A schoolmate of Dhuvik's had called them over to his family's fire, inviting them to eat with the other guests.

Now the three boys sat among warriors, listening closely to the latest news that trickled in along the hard-ridden post roads and flashed from *yurt* to *yurt*.

"Inaldjuk did not put the gift-bearers into prison," the warrior answered Dhuvik's question. "He let them depart, but sent his soldiers to the caravansary. They saw the great riches that came from our Khan's empire, and demanded much of it, saying Inaldjuk had not been honored with fitting gifts."

Another warrior, his large strong hand gripping the hilt of his sword, took up the tale. "These demands were refused, and our leader with two other men went once more to Inaldjuk, to protest the attempted thievery. Inaldjuk put them in prison, and ordered his soldiers to seize our caravan."

"It is said that two of our men managed to escape from the caravansary," the host added, "though the rest were taken captive. One rode to a post station with the news, and the other reached Kaban, who was then at Samarkand."

Dhuvik spoke then. "My father left his caravan in charge of armed guards outside Samarkand." The warriors listened to Dhuvik, for they knew the Khan had sent word to Chentai of the part her husband played in the crisis. "He went at once to Urgendj, and reported the theft of the caravan to Shah Ala-u-Din. But Inaldjuk had already sent a message to the court, claiming our caravans were filled with spies."

"It is a coward who stoops to lying," a warrior muttered angrily, voicing the thoughts of those around him. "What then, Dhuvik? I have not heard the whole story."

"My father argued well and in truth," Dhuvik said proudly. "At last the Shah agreed that he was not certain our merchants were spies. But he put off the discussion, saying he would speak to my father the next day."

"Was it then Kaban and the two with him were put in prison?" a warrior asked.

"Not in prison," Dhuvik corrected. "They were treated as guests, yet many armed guards appeared, saying they were to keep them from harm at the hands of angry Khoresmians. That night they escaped, and each rode a different way to warn the caravan near Samarkand and the ones on the way to Kabul and Meshed."

"It was then the remaining three caravans turned back," a soldier added. "I hear they are on their way now, taking the hardest passes in the mountains so they cannot be easily discovered or followed. Does Kaban return with them?"

"Not until all three caravans are out of danger," Dhuvik answered. "Then he will gallop ahead to make a full report to the Khan."

"Can any of you say when our troops move against Khoresm?" asked a warrior. "I am eager to avenge this insult!"

"Word has been sent throughout the empire," another answered. "We will be ready to march in two months."

"When the snow flies," said another thoughtfully. "And there is ice in the passes."

"Genghis Khan is not going to wait until spring," rejoined the first warrior. "His anger is great enough to level the mountains we must cross."

And though it was the custom to refrain from battle during the cold months, the warriors approved of the winter march.

Darkness fell, but still Karakorum talked of the coming war. Dhuvik and Jalair left their host's fire, and accompanied by Dhuvik's friend, began visiting other cadets. All the boys hoped they might take part in the campaign, for often student officers were permitted to fight at their fathers' sides.

Jalair was depressed by the talk of war, and saying he was tired, left Dhuvik with his friends and returned to Kaban's *yurt*.

The *yurt* was deserted, the servants having gone out to hear the latest news. Jalair sat on a cushion and moodily poked up the fire.

So far since the news of the incident at Otrar, no one had shown by word or glance that Jalair was considered an enemy. The excitement of war momentarily had driven every thought from their minds, save that of the coming struggle. Perhaps, too, Karakorum was so accustomed to seeing Jalair in the cloak of the Khan's Hawker that few remembered the country of his birth.

But Yatu would remember, and would remember, too, when Arrow's claws raked so near, and when Jalair held in his hands the loosened leash of a Golden Hawk.

With a stab of fear, Jalair recalled the trade festival when he had won the hawk trials. He heard again his bold words, daring to ask for a pair of the Golden Hawks. Again he saw the alarming look on Genghis Khan's face, softened by Yatu's words.

Now there would be no mitigating words from Yatu. Instead, the scarred warrior would be quick to seize on the war as an excuse to avenge himself on Jalair.

The fire flickered low and Jalair put on more thorns from a nearby pile. The flames leaped hungrily, their red light glowing on Kaban's armor hanging along the sloping walls of the *yurt*.

Kaban had put off his war dress for the peaceful purpose of trade. Now he would again wear the lacquered leather breastplates and the steel-plated helmet with its white horsetail crest. And he would swing his huge curved sword at

Khoresmian foes. Dhuvik would be there too, perhaps riding beside his father. Chentai would remain at home, caring for the herds and conducting the family affairs, taking Kaban's place until her warrior husband and son came home.

Only Jalair would be missing from the family circle.

He was an enemy now, and his place was either in Samarkand, or in a prison *yurt*. He would have to learn once more to hate all Mongols.

Angrily, Jalair thrust aside these thoughts. Iskander was in great danger, as was he himself.

He thought he could count on Karakorum's excitement for another day. During this time, guards would be a little less alert than usual.

Perhaps Iskander could think of a way to escape. If only Jalair could visit him without arousing suspicion, they might arrange the rescue together.

For a long time Jalair turned over in his mind dozens of excuses to see the captive, and cast each one aside. He could not offer to persuade Iskander to turn traitor, since the Khan publicly claimed to have no interest in traitors. Nor would explaining the Otrar incident be a good excuse, for the guards might fear the news would make the prisoner desperate for escape. Iskander was fed every day, so Jalair could hardly offer his services. Besides, he must not appear to be too sympathetic with a supposed traitor.

It grew quite late, and though the city was still very much awake, Jalair thought Dhuvik or Chentai might return soon. He had no wish to talk of the coming war.

He went through the curtain that separated his sleeping room from the rest of the *yurt*, his problem still unsolved.

Then, just before sleep claimed him, he found the answer. He remembered that Iskander was a Moslem.

There was no moon, but the stars shone brightly in the black sky. Now and then a breeze yawed across the few sand dunes that scalloped the southern margin of the grassy plains surrounding Karakorum.

Jalair burrowed deeper in his sheepskin-lined jacket. In spite of the warm days, Karakorum nights were growing cold with the season's advance. The two horses stamped restlessly and pulled at their picket lines, anxious to warm themselves by moving around as they did in the herds.

Iskander was late. The escape had been set for an hour after moondown.

Just then a new sound echoed through the whistle of the night wind and the mutter of shifting sands.

Perhaps the ruse had been discovered after all, Jalair thought with a chill of dread.

The events of the day flashed through his mind as he searched for errors in his plan.

That morning Jalair had lingered at the breakfast fire, saying Idikut would surely excuse his late arrival because of the news of war. Dhuvik's classes had been cancelled, and he had only to wait for the special meeting of the cadet officers that afternoon. Chentai had been glad for the opportunity of a long leisurely talk with her "two sons."

And so the three had talked of pasturage and herds, the wonders of Cathay, hunting during the steppe's varied seasons, ancient legends, and—briefly—of the coming war.

Chentai smiled when Jalair begged her to sing one of the old Mongol lays. She called for a lute, and taking it into her silk-gowned lap, picked out a delicate tune.

As the notes of the song died away, Jalair knew he would never hear Chentai sing again, nor join in with her infectious laughter.

"And now, go to the mews," Chentai said. "You must not be too late."

Jalair savored the crisp morning air as he trotted to his work. People he knew greeted him with a friendly call or a cheerful wave as he passed.

Idikut had already cleaned the mews when he arrived. Jalair remembered each word of advice and every line of instruction that Idikut offered that morning as they worked side by side.

"Winter is soon upon us," Idikut said as they ate the midday meal together. "This morning I saw the first of the wild hawks migrating south."

With a sudden pang, Jalair remembered the hawks he had

helped train that summer. He could not bear to leave without seeing them in flight for the last time. "Are we going to release the hawks today?"

"No," said Idikut. "I must first select the few younger ones that I feel might be able to stand the winter in the mews. But we must release the older birds, Jalair. They do poorly in the mews over the winter, and will not hunt well next summer."

"I know," Jalair answered. Even the younger hawks that were sometimes kept through the cold period often failed to develop well. The Golden Hawks were the only breed that could thrive when kept entirely in a mews. "The hawks must be released soon to join the migration. But Idikut, can we not fly them for the last time today?"

The Hawk Master smiled. "Very well. We will take them out this afternoon."

As they rode out to the plains that afternoon, with their field cadges on the saddles before them, the cool wind held a promise of early snow. Already the hawks were restless with the urge to migrate to the warmer southlands.

One by one they sent up the hawks. Peregrine, goshawk, gyrfalcon took their turn in the sky. Lanner and saker ringed up, well-trained and perfect in flight. The falcon and tiercel of each breed stretched their wings. Branchers and haggards—flying for man for the last time. Unless, perhaps, some should voluntarily return to the mews next spring as sometimes happened.

But for Jalair there was no returning.

That evening Idikut went to care for the Golden Hawks, leaving Jalair to place the mews in good order for the night.

For the last time, Jalair fed and watered the hawks, then went to each one in turn to stroke the sleek feathers before leaving the mews.

He trotted directly to the prison *yurt*. Karakorum had not yet settled down from the announcement of war, for all day fresh news came over the post roads and must be discussed. The guards did not seem to think it strange when Jalair dismounted before the black *yurt*.

"When I was here last," Jalair told them, remembering every word of his carefully worked out speech, "Iskander asked that I might see him again soon. Since he is a Moslem, he wishes me to recite words from the Koran, that he may be comforted in his captivity."

All educated Khoresmians knew the Koran by heart, but the Mongols would not know this. Jalair passed the guards easily and entered the darkened *yurt*.

"What is all that shouting of the past day?" Iskander cried out in Arabic. "I have heard Otrar named."

"It is I, Iskander," Jalair said in Turki, fumbling for the lamp. He struck his fire-striker, and soon the lamp flamed.

Iskander's eyes studied him. "Have you been sent here?"

"No. I told the guards you wished me to recite the Koran."

"What is this about Otrar?"

Jalair told him of Inaldjuk's seizure of the Mongol caravan and the Khan's declaration of war on Khoresm.

"Then I am lost!" Iskander moaned, moving his head restlessly in the *kang* that imprisoned his neck and wrists. "They will kill me."

"I can give you a chance," Jalair said. "And I can get two horses. But I do not know how you can get out of this prison *yurt* without giving rise to alarm."

"Two horses?" Iskander asked eagerly. "Then you are going with me?"

"Yes, if you can escape the city."

"I can find a way to leave this *yurt*," Iskander promised.

Jalair unsheathed his knife and began working. A wooden peg wedged through two iron staples fastened the unhinged end of the *kang*. It was this wooden peg that Jalair began cutting through.

"I'm going to cut this peg until only a splinter of wood holds the *kang* shut," he explained as he worked. "When you want to get free, you can strike the end of the *kang* on the ground and the peg will snap."

"When and where shall we meet?"

"Do you remember the plains south of Karakorum?"

Iskander nodded as much as the *kang* would let him. "I noted the area well when I was brought here."

"Some distance west of the road into Karakorum there is a great pillar of rock. It is just where the grass gives way to sand dunes. Next to it is a rocky ridge—a fine hiding place. I will be there with the horses. Can you meet me an hour after the moon sets?"

Iskander nodded again, and Jalair put out the lamp.

"One moment," the captive said. "Give me the Mongol word for 'physician.'"

"Are you ill?" Jalair asked in alarm.

"Not too ill to flee from Genghis Khan."

It was almost dark when Jalair reached the *yurt* of Kaban. Chentai and Dhuvik were finishing the evening meal. Jalair touched little of his food, and to Chentai's question, answered that he was tired and would go to sleep early.

Lying in his felt blankets behind the curtain, he heard Chentai dismiss the servants for the night before she went out. A schoolmate of Dhuvik's came in, and shortly both boys left. The *yurt* of Kaban fell into silence except for the distant mutter of a restless city.

Jalair rose and stole out of the *yurt*. He slipped through the crowded streets, passed the ring of *kibitkas* and camel carts that edged the city, then walked quickly over the dark plains until he found Kaban's horse herds.

There were herdsmen guarding the animals, but so well

did Jalair know their movements and habits that he was able to slip away with two of Kaban's horses without being seen or heard.

He tied them to a *kibitka* at the edge of the city, then went back to Kaban's *yurt* for saddles, bridles, and food supplies for the long journey to Khoresm. He looked over his possessions and picked out the few things necessary for the trip. The blue cloak with the silver hawk he folded neatly, hesitated, then left behind. He could hardly approach Shah Ala-u-Din in the cloak of Genghis Khan's Hawker.

In the shadows of the *kibitkas*, far from revealing campfires, Jalair prepared the horses for the escape. He was about to lead them to the meeting place when he thought of the Golden Hawks.

They were the reason for his long journey to Karakorum, and now he was leaving them behind.

Impulsively, Jalair retied the two horses, and taking a circuitous route, slipped up to the mews of the Golden Hawks without being seen by anyone who knew him.

The mews was dark since Yatu was at the council, and Jalair lit the small sheep-fat lamp. The hawks' feathers seemed the color of beaten copper in the light of the flames.

Jalair went directly to the pair that he knew, from helping Idikut, were the best. Quickly he unleashed the falcon and fitted her with a sock. He found a small carrying basket, and placed the female inside one of the compartments. Then he untied the tiercel, put a falcon sock on, and placed him in the basket with the falcon.

He raided Yatu's stores for extra gear, and packed a leather bag with food for the hawks. These items also went into the basket. He snuffed out the lamp.

Jalair would bring the Golden Hawk back to Shah Ala-u-Din. He himself would be made Hawker to the Shah. And the promise Jalair had made to the memory of his father would be kept.

Yet Genghis Khan would still have the Goldens too. And Yatu would handle them until Torgul returned.

Jalair's task was only half done.

He set down the basket and went to the mews of the Khan's hawks, taking great care not to be noticed. Here, he did not strike a light, for he knew every inch of the mews. He unleashed the largest and fiercest goshawk, Bayan's haggard falcon, and lifting her to his gauntleted fist, returned to the Golden Hawks.

By the light of the sheep-fat lamp which he rekindled, Jalair found an old leash Yatu had discarded. With this worn leather strap, Jalair fastened the goshawk to one of the long perching bars that ran along the *yurt* walls. His last act was to remove the hood from the goshawk.

He put out the lamp, slung the basket strap over his shoulder and slipped back to the horses.

By the time the goshawk tore free from the brittle leash, he and Iskander would be galloping to freedom.

Jalair hated to kill the remaining Goldens. Yet it was the only way he could devise to keep the fruits of Darien's efforts out of Mongol hands.

Though the moon had not yet set, many riders were entering and leaving Karakorum as men gathered to discuss the news and left to spread it. Jalair was only another horseman, and no sentry challenged him.

Quickly he found the outcropping of rock that marked the meeting place. Now he had only to wait for Iskander.

The moon turned in the sky, sank below the horizon, and an hour passed. Jalair began to wonder if Iskander had managed to slip out of the prison *yurt*.

And then came the grating sound as of a boot on rock.

Jalair froze, thinking over his movements and trying to invent an excuse for them should the noise maker prove to be a sentry.

For a moment, the stars shining over the rim of rock were blotted out by a dark figure. Then they reappeared as the cloaked visitor slid down near Jalair.

"Here I am, Jalair," came Iskander's harsh whisper.

Jalair had not realized how frightened he had been until relief flooded through him. "The horses are over here. How did you escape?"

"I called for a physician," Iskander explained in a low tone. "I broke open the *kang,* and when the physician appeared, I knocked him unconscious. In his robes I walked out and through the city. I proceeded with dignity as befits a physician, and for this reason I am late."

They mounted their horses and walked them toward the nearest mountains, lest any echo of hoofs bring guards upon them.

Once in the mountains, Iskander broke their silence. "Which way to Khoresm?"

"I know only one road," Jalair said. "Southwest to the Takla Makan."

"A good route," Iskander approved. "The Mongols will not expect us to cross that desert."

They felt their way cautiously up into the mountains, following rivers that had cut passes out of the ancient rock. The Golden Hawks in the basket tied to Jalair's saddle were uncomplaining, for they were frequently carried in this manner.

When dawn felt its silvery way through the sky, they were well within the vast Altai range that bounded the western edge of the Gobi Desert.

During the next three days they wound through the rugged peaks, trotting often and galloping across every level stretch. They drank from the cold streams, and ate their food as they rode, for they could risk neither time to cook meals nor the fire that might lead the Mongols toward them.

On the morning of the fourth day, while the sun reddened the mountaintops at their backs, they wound down out of the Altai's western foothills. Before them lay the dread Takla Makan, a desert vastness little traveled except by occasional Mongol caravans during the short time of peaceful trade with Khoresm.

Jalair reined up and turned toward the jagged peaks of the Altai for a last look at the hills that had meant home.

13 Wasteland

"How long can the horses go without grass?" Iskander wanted to know. "It has been two days now."

"About another day, if we ride them slowly," Jalair answered, searching the sunset-reddened desert for a hint of the precious green. "But we will reach the Lop Nor late tomorrow night where there will be good grazing for them around the lake."

"And better food for us," Iskander grumbled.

Jalair was about to answer, but thinking better of it, trotted along in silence, the thick barren sand muffling the horses' hoofs.

Jalair had packed enough trail rations to last both of them until they reached Khotan, if they ate sparingly. There was the dried meat that Jalair each night soaked in water and boiled, risking a small fire now that they were in the desert. And every morning he placed dried milk and water in a leather sack, the jogging of the horses churning it to a smooth liquid in time for the midday meal. There was millet and rice, dried fruits and nuts. And once there had been water enough to take them halfway across the Takla Makan before refilling the leather bottles from distant rivers or wells.

But Iskander could not confine himself to a day's rations after a week of prison food. His appetite had reduced their supplies to barely enough to take them to the Lop Nor. Though willingly enough he had eaten what Jalair prepared for them, he had complained continually of the food. "In the Shah's court," he had been fond of reminding Jalair, "we would not give such food to the dogs."

Travel had become faster once they had reached the monotonous level of the Takla Makan. Within three swift days they had crossed the caravan trail near Qomul, passing it within a half-day's gallop during the night.

After that, the grass began thinning rapidly, and fewer animals started up at their horses' approach, for they were now in the terrible wasteland with its goblin sounds that made all men fear the vast Takla Makan. During the last

two days, the horses found scant forage. Jalair was glad they were only a full day's ride from the Lop Nor.

"What is the Lop Nor?" Iskander had asked when Jalair described the route they would take.

"It is a lake formed by the Tarim River," Jalair had told him. He was retracing the route Kaban's caravan had taken when first he journeyed to the land of Genghis Khan.

Though Kaban had left the Tarim River where it turned south to form the Lop Nor, Jalair clearly remembered Dhuvik's casual directions to the desert lake.

"From the Lop Nor, we will follow the Tarim River north, then take the Khotan River all the way to Khotan," Jalair added.

"The Tarim River?" Iskander repeated. "The Mongol post road passes close to it at one point, for that is the way they took me to Karakorum."

"Where the river touches the post road, it also splits into many streams that part and come together farther upstream. We will follow the branch farthest from the post road, and so will not be seen."

"It will not go well with you if you plan to warn the Mongols," Iskander threatened.

"I am a Khoresmian, as you are!" Jalair answered angrily. "How dare you say you do not trust me?"

"Of course, I trust you," Iskander soothed. "I was but testing your loyalty."

Now they were only a day's ride from the Lop Nor. The lack of food did not bother Jalair, for once in the lush grazing grounds of the lake and the rivers that would follow, the Golden Hawks could hunt for them. Indeed, he was glad that the hawks would prove their worth, for Iskander had at first complained of them.

"If we are caught," Iskander had pointed out while they were still in the Altai, "our fate will be worse for having stolen the Khan's hawks."

"I will not go to Shah Ala-u-Din without them," Jalair had replied. "We must keep the Goldens with us, for this is the last pair alive."

"What do you mean?" Iskander had asked sharply.

"The other Goldens are dead," Jalair had told him. "I set a goshawk on them the night we escaped."

"Foolish boy!" Iskander had cried. "Why give the Mongols more reason to track us down and slay us? Just to bring the Shah your idea of a fitting gift!"

"But they are no gift," Jalair had insisted. "I am returning them to Shah Ala-u-Din."

"Of course. I forgot," Iskander had said. "But it was still a foolish deed."

Now, however, Iskander would be glad of having the hawks along.

The intense sun shining on the sands of the Takla Makan made Jalair's eyes hurt, but he squinted ahead in his continual search for some forage for the horses. Though another day's ride would bring them to Lop Nor's grass, Jalair did not want the horses to be so weak they would have to linger an extra day or two beside the lake.

The horses sensed the forage before Jalair could even make out a green patch in the blue dune-shadows cast by the setting sun. Both mounts whinnied, and started forward eagerly.

"Is it grass?" asked Iskander, giving his mount his head.

"I think so," Jalair answered. "But I can see nothing yet."

The horses veered to the left and cantered straight toward the promise of food. It was not long before they came to a great patch of low leafy plants, and the horses eagerly dropped their heads as the travelers dismounted.

"Make the evening meal, Jalair," Iskander ordered. "The horses can graze meanwhile."

Jalair unsaddled both horses and set about his work. Though it annoyed him that Iskander never helped with the trail work, he remembered that it was considered a disgrace for a member of Shah Ala-u-Din's court to work with his hands. It was for this reason that Kurush, Iskander, and the Shah himself had refused to let Jalair become a hawker.

By the time they had eaten and Jalair had cleaned up their camp, night had blackened the desert sky. A million stars twinkled brilliantly overhead, except where the moon's sickle blotted out their light with a stronger glow.

"We have a long ride ahead tomorrow before we reach the Lop Nor," Jalair said. "Perhaps we can ride on two or three hours before we stop for the night."

"I am just beginning to feel rested," Iskander protested. There was a moment's silence, and Jalair knew Iskander was thinking of the lush game the hawks could catch when they arrived at their destination. "Very well," Iskander agreed. "Let us ride on."

Jalair resaddled the horses and packed on the supplies, being careful to tie securely his basket of hawks. The horses seemed sluggish after their first full meal in two days, and Jalair suggested they walk them, since trotting was hard for them on a full stomach.

They had not gone very far when Iskander's mount stumbled awkwardly, nearly throwing him out of his saddle. "My horse has developed a rough walk," Iskander complained. "Let me have your mount."

Jalair changed horses with him, and indeed he had never been on a horse that walked so clumsily. Twice his mount's lurches nearly spilled him from the saddle.

"Your horse is no better," said Iskander. "I am accustomed to the fine mounts of the Shah's stable."

"Perhaps we should let them rest from their meal," Jalair said. "We can continue later."

"What!" exclaimed the courtier. "And make me lose an hour of precious sleep? We will go on."

The horses stumbled on through the moon-drenched dunes. They walked slower and slower, and at last Jalair's mount stopped. He dismounted, and, tugging gently at the reins, urged his horse forward. But the animal refused to move, standing with lowered head, blowing as if from a hard run.

Suddenly the horse gave a great shuddering gasp, and lunged forward to the ground. Jalair worked hard to get the animal to rise, but the horse did not move.

Iskander came running back on foot. "My horse dropped to the ground and will not move!"

Jalair stood up from his mount. "He is dead."

"But why? What is it?"

Jalair searched for a reason, and remembered Kaban's men driving horses away from a patch of foliage. "The plants they ate must have been poison."

Iskander clutched his arm. "If you knew that, why did you let them eat?"

"I did not know it!" Jalair cried, pulling away. "Dhuvik once tried to show me the difference between good and poisonous graze, but I could not tell."

There was a long silence while the full significance of this tragedy grew upon them.

"Take off the supplies," Iskander finally ordered. "We will camp not far from here."

The next morning as the sun shot its fiery beams across the sands, Jalair was the first to awaken. He looked around for the horses, and then, with a stab of shock, he remembered what had happened.

Quickly he built a fire and boiled a little rice for his breakfast. Then he unpacked the needles and thread hawkers use for sewing leather hoods, and, taking the saddle blankets, he cut and stitched until he had fashioned two packs such as beggars and wandering minstrels wore on their backs. Just as he finished sewing on the last shoulder strap, Iskander awoke, demanding his breakfast.

"How long will it take us to walk to the Lop Nor?" Iskander asked when he finished eating.

Jalair was busy packing the supplies into the back packs, but he paused to calculate. "About three days."

Iskander's eyes opened in fright. "And the food?"

"We have enough for a day and a half. If we go on half rations, we can last until the Lop Nor. There I will send the Goldens after game." He stared at Iskander's rigid expression, and then he saw that the courtier was terrified. "There is no need to worry. We have plenty of water."

He handed Iskander his pack, and the courtier struggled into the shoulder straps, the physician's robes making it an awkward task. Jalair strapped the basket containing the hawks to his waist beneath his own pack, and they started off.

All day they walked steadily. Only once did Iskander speak. "Perhaps the hawks can find game."

"Not in this wasteland," Jalair answered, shifting his pack to a more comfortable position.

The food that might have taken them to the haven of the Lop Nor lasted only that day. Iskander could never think of tomorrow, and in his imagination he was already starving. That night Jalair surveyed the empty food sacks in disgust, but said nothing. Luckily he kept the hawks' rations in the basket, and he fed the birds after Iskander had gone to sleep rolled up in a blanket on the sand.

The next morning, Jalair took up a notch in his thick leather belt, then went to help Iskander shoulder his pack, for the courtier was struggling impatiently with his flowing robes. But Iskander made no move to begin the day's march. "Send up the hawks," he urged. "Perhaps they can find a little game."

"It would do no good," Jalair explained. "This is the worst part of the Takla Makan, and even desert animals avoid it. Besides, the hawks might be seen. Let us go on, for every step brings us closer to Lop Nor."

But Iskander would have none of it. "I cannot travel on an empty stomach. Surely a boy who hopes to be Hawker to Shah Ala-u-Din can fetch game even in a wasteland. I must have food, I tell you."

So Jalair opened the basket and slipped Valiant, the tiercel,

out of the falcon sock. He put on his gauntlet, and gently backed the male hawk on his fist. Then he unhooded, and jerked his wrist forward, the leash running free through the ring of the jesses as the Golden flew off.

The tiercel stroked his great golden wings and spiraled quickly to his pitch, the jingle of the tiny bells on his legs growing fainter as the hawk ringed upward.

For a long time, the tiercel waited on, wheeling and wheeling as Jalair and Iskander watched anxiously. And as Jalair studied the flashes of gold where the sun struck the tiercel's feathers, it came to him with a sudden thrill. He, the son of Darien, was flying the Golden Hawk!

Iskander rudely brought him back to earth. "If these Goldens of yours cannot fetch game, they are no fitting gift for Shah Ala-u-Din."

"There is no game," Jalair answered hotly. "And I told you once before that the Goldens are no gift. I am returning them to the Shah."

They continued to wait as the tiercel circled at his pitch, but not once did Valiant so much as dip a wing.

"Send up the falcon," Iskander ordered impatiently. "She will be the better hunter of the pair."

"The Golden tiercel is finer than even a peregrine falcon. It is simply that there is no game."

It was with a great show of annoyance that Iskander finally permitted Jalair to call the tiercel to fist. At last they started the day's march.

But their steady pace toward Lop Nor with its waiting water and game was interrupted frequently by Iskander ordering the hawks into the air again and again. Throughout the long hungry day, Jalair had to keep the hawks raking across the sky. Valiant and Empress took their turns in the fruitless search for game, until their weariness made Jalair call them to hand in spite of Iskander's protests.

When the sun was just touching its fiery rim to the horizon, Iskander threw off his pack. "I cannot go a step farther until I have eaten!"

Jalair considered boiling up the hawks' rations, but that would last Iskander one meal. The Goldens had to eat in order to hunt, and to live.

"Perhaps after an hour or two of sleep, we can continue walking tonight," Jalair suggested. "Hunger is always sharpest when a person is tired."

"I shall be yet hungrier in two more hours," Iskander grumbled.

Jalair ignored the complaint and rolled himself up in his blanket. He shut his eyes against the setting sun, but his thoughts were far from sleep. When night had completely darkened the desert, and Iskander was asleep, he would get up and feed the hawks.

After a long time, though the sunset still shone through his closed eyes, Jalair heard Iskander call softly, "Jalair, are you asleep?"

Jalair did not answer, for a conversation with Iskander would delay the hawks' meal.

Suddenly Jalair heard the familiar creak which the wicker basket gave when its lid was lifted. He threw aside his blanket and sprang up.

Iskander held Valiant in his hand. The sunset's bloody glow added a fiery gleam to the knife that flashed out and down.

"No!" Jalair screamed, lunging for Iskander.

The courtier evaded him easily, and laughed as he held up the dead tiercel, its golden breast stained with crimson. "These hawks will be good for something after all. Build a fire at once."

Jalair's head spun with anger and horror, and he could not move.

Iskander started a fire of the tough desert thorn, and the tiny flames became the focus of Jalair's hatred.

The tiercel was quickly stripped of its proud plumage, then the carcass was cleaned and hung on a makeshift spit above the fire. Iskander sniffed greedily at the roasting hawk, but the odor made Jalair ill.

Sick at heart, Jalair bent to the basket and took out the falcon. He sat watching Iskander at the fire, cuddling Empress in his lap. The scent of her mate's blood made Empress nervous, and Jalair stroked her protectively.

He saw the fire and the roasting hawk, saw the bloodstained golden feathers on the sands. Yet shock so froze his mind that he sat numbly, not quite able to grasp what had happened.

Iskander drew his knife, cut away the tiercel's roasted leg and began eating. "Will you not join me?" he mocked as he chewed lustily.

The sight was too much for Jalair. "The strain is lost!" he cried in agony. "Do you understand what that means? This was the last pair of Goldens alive—and now the greatest hawk in the world is lost!"

Iskander shrugged as he munched on a wing. "A bird is food." He paused and studied the falcon in Jalair's hands. "I will have Empress for tomorrow's meal."

"And what will be food when the falcon is gone?" Jalair raged.

"A man of opportunity, such as myself, can always find some way," Iskander answered easily. The courtier ate rapidly, and though the tiercel was a large bird, soon nothing remained but the tooth-polished bones. Iskander licked his fingers, stamped out the fire, and rolled up in his blanket.

Still Jalair hunched on the sand, stroking and comforting Empress for the loss of her mate.

More than a hawk had been eaten. Iskander's vicious teeth had gnawed away Jalair's pledge to his dead father—a pledge that had kept Darien's memory alive and clear. And there were Darien's years of patient labor and use of his great knowledge painstakingly acquired—years of careful selection and breeding until at last the finest hawk man could produce had spread its golden wings in the sky.

Yet Empress remained. No longer a member of a proud strain was she, but only a curiosity.

Slowly a great resolve swelled in Jalair's heart. Darien had started with nothing, but Jalair held in his hands the last Golden Hawk. It was a better beginning than his father had.

At all costs, he must preserve that precious beginning.

Jalair slept fitfully through the long night, waking from time to time to open the basket in his arms. Empress was still in her snug compartment. Sometimes she wakened too, and Jalair rubbed his finger over her fine head feathers.

He watched the pale dawn spread over the cold sands, and slept no more. When Iskander stirred, Jalair took

Empress from her basket and flung her into the gray sky. "Wait on!" he commanded, letting her understand she must not come down until he gave the word. This was the test of the great intelligence that Darien had bred into the Golden Hawk—a bird of prey that could be taught commands. Though he hated the thought of the Goldens in Mongol hands, Jalair was glad now they had at least kept up the strain well, and trained them perfectly.

Iskander threw off his blanket and, as Jalair had expected, went straight to the wicker basket. Jalair smiled at his wrathful mutter as Iskander dropped the empty basket and turned his eyes upward to the circling falcon.

"It matters little," Iskander muttered, "for the hawk must alight sometime." He waited until the sun was full above the horizon. Then he took from the basket the dried meat and milk curds he had seen inside. "Boil this," he ordered Jalair.

Iskander ate the hawk rations, the while keeping an alert eye on the circling falcon. "If your Empress sights game, she can yet save her life." At last he shouldered his pack. "We cannot wait here all day. Call the falcon to hand."

Jalair stubbornly refused, though Iskander's narrowed eyes held a threat.

They started out through the desert, and to Jalair's glad surprise, Empress shifted her circles so that she was always overhead.

"If we walk all night," Jalair began hopefully, "we can be at the Lop Nor a day sooner."

Iskander did not bother to answer.

Somehow the long tiring day passed. Jalair kept Empress waiting on at her high pitch, her golden pinions flashing in the sun. Several times the weary falcon wavered, anxious to be called to the fist and puzzled at the long wait-on. Her master flushed no game for her talons, nor did he swing the training lure. Three times when Empress began to spiral downward, Jalair waved her off, crying, "Wait on!" Three times the golden falcon checked her descent, and beat upward to resume her patient circling.

Several times through the terrible journey, Jalair lagged far behind Iskander. As he silently held out his fist, the falcon stooped to the welcome perch. He was able to carry her for a few restful moments before Iskander would chance to turn, his hand flashing to his dagger when he saw the falcon so near. Then again Jalair's fist would shoot out, launching Empress back to her post in the sky.

Now it was nearly sunset.

Jalair noted the high outcropping of rock they passed. Perhaps he could hide the weary falcon in its crevices after Iskander fell asleep.

They had not walked far beyond the ridge of sand-scoured rock when Iskander swung his pack to the ground and announced they would camp there for the night.

Jalair followed Iskander's glance skyward. The nearly exhausted falcon was circling lower. Iskander looked at Jalair with a triumphant smile before he rolled himself in his blanket.

The sun had already dipped below the horizon, leaving behind a fiery glow, when Jalair finally dared hold out his gauntleted fist. Eagerly the falcon alighted and let Jalair stroke her sleek feathers.

Suddenly a strong hand clutched Jalair's shoulder and spun him around.

Iskander had not been asleep after all!

Jalair threw the falcon from his fist. "Fly, Empress!"

The Golden Hawk fluttered wearily to the ground. Before Jalair could wrench free from Iskander's grasp, the courtier flung him aside and jumped toward the falcon. His raised knife caught the red gleam of the setting sun.

In an instant Jalair was on him, while the tired hawk fluttered a little distance away. Iskander turned on Jalair, the sharp point of the knife pressed against the boy's jacket.

"Look!" cried Jalair, trying to point behind Iskander.

"You will not trick me that way!"

"She has sighted game."

The weary falcon had summoned forth the last of her strength and was now ringing upward.

Iskander risked a glance backward, then dropped his arms.

The falcon's pitch was not high, for she had sensed her prey and needed altitude only for the last desperate plunge.

Empress turned on one pointed wing and began her stoop.

"Where is she going?" Iskander demanded.

"Over there," Jalair pointed. "Behind that ridge of rock we passed."

Together they ran toward the craggy cliff-like mass. Empress had disappeared behind it, and now they saw her rise and plunge again and again.

"Must be a large animal," Jalair panted.

Iskander reached the ridge first and disappeared behind it. Jalair ran hard after him, then stopped short.

Though the outcropping of rock cast a massive shadow, Jalair could make out a horse, and beside it was a figure stretched on the ground. Iskander, who had found rope somewhere, was busy tying the wrists of the unconscious figure.

"It is a Mongol," Iskander said, knotting the rope heavily to be certain the prisoner could not escape. "He was busy fighting the falcon from his horse, and did not hear me come up behind him."

"Is it Yatu?" Jalair asked, for an instant forgetting Empress who patiently waited to be called to hand.

Iskander turned the captive over. There was enough light in the evening sky for Jalair to make out his features.

"Why," he gasped in astonishment. "It is Dhuvik!"

14 The Beat of Wings

Iskander glanced at him sharply. "So this is a friend of yours. I have heard you mention the name before."

Quickly Jalair added, "I have seen him about in Karakorum." But he could see Iskander had not forgotten his astonished cry of recognition and the ring of concern it held.

Iskander dragged the unconscious Dhuvik to the base of the mass of rock. "Take provisions from his horse and make a meal," he ordered.

Jalair did so, first hooding Empress and tethering her on a rock ledge far up. Soon he finished preparing the meal and as he was about to sit down to eat, Iskander came up to him and whipped Jalair's knife from its sheath.

"I will keep your knife for you," Iskander explained with a grin, "so you will not be moved to a foolish act by some burst of compassion for our captive."

They ate in silence, Jalair's anxious eyes going to Dhuvik's still form from time to time.

After Jalair cleared up the remains of the meal, he fed Empress.

"Your precious hawk is safe for a while," Iskander said, watching him. "Now unsaddle the horse and picket him. Throw any weapons you find in a pile on the ground."

Jalair bent to this task under Iskander's watchful eyes. There was no chance for him to hide any weapon, so he put Dhuvik's bow and arrows and short lance on the ground next to the sword and knife Iskander had already taken from the prisoner. He picketed the horse, then, at Iskander's direction, made a bed of blankets for the courtier.

He began unrolling blankets for himself when he felt a rope drop over him, pinning his arms to his sides. Iskander pulled his wrists together behind his back and bound them tightly.

"What are you doing?" Jalair cried angrily.

"I have no wish to awaken tomorrow and find you and your friend gone."

"He is no friend of mine," Jalair told him.

"We shall see."

Iskander pushed him to the ground and tied his legs together. By the faint glow of embers from the fire, Jalair watched Iskander place all of Dhuvik's weapons in his clothing, wrapping the full robes closely and tying his waist with a sash. Then Iskander kicked out the dying fire, and Jalair heard him roll up in the blankets, the weapons scraping together beneath the robes. No sharpened blade could be taken without Iskander being awakened.

Behind him came a faint moan.

Jalair worked his arms and legs, hunching over to Dhuvik at the base of the rock outcrop. The night was black, but Dhuvik's moans guided him until he sat next to his friend.

"Are you awake, Dhuvik?"

"Jalair, it is you!" Dhuvik had been knocked unconscious before Jalair had run around the rock ridge. Now he pushed himself into a sitting position. "Has he tied you up, too?"

"Yes, and then he put all your weapons and my knife in his robes. He is lying on them now."

They spoke in whispers, for Iskander might be lying awake to stop any plans the boys might design for freeing themselves.

"I am glad you are safe," Dhuvik said. "I was afraid that Iskander might have harmed you. Though I did not see who struck me from behind, it could be none other than Iskander, for I was trailing you both."

"True, I am alive," Jalair agreed. "But I am not certain of my safety. He knows I know you, for I could not help but cry your name when I saw you on the ground. Are there others behind you?"

"I traveled alone," Dhuvik sighed. "The telling of that tale can wait. Can we untie each other?"

They pressed their backs together, the fingers of each working at the knots of the other.

Jalair's fingers began to ache in the unnatural position. He stopped now and then and wriggled them back to life. But though they worked a long time, not a single knot had been loosened.

With Jalair's struggles, the ropes binding his wrists began cutting into his skin, and at last he was forced to stop entirely.

"The rope is firm, and well-seasoned," Jalair complained.

"Indeed, it is fine rope," Dhuvik agreed ruefully. "Made by the best rope-maker in Karakorum, and said to hold the wildest horse. With it, I planned to capture Iskander."

"Perhaps we can bring our hands in front of us, and use our teeth," Jalair suggested.

They set to work, straining to bring their bound hands under their legs and around their feet.

After a long sweating struggle, Dhuvik said, "It would work if our feet were not tied together."

"Or if Iskander had left some slack between our wrists," Jalair added.

They lay panting on the sands, and then Dhuvik hunched back to the wall of rock behind them. "Try rubbing the rope against the rock."

Jalair doubted if it would work, yet he followed Dhuvik's example. Though the bulk of the rock mass from the top down had been scoured into sharp edges by the constant grind of wind-blown sand, the base had been but recently uncovered by the shifting desert and so was smooth.

"The rock has worn away my skin," Jalair sighed after a time. "Yet the rope is as firm as ever."

Exhausted as the boys were with their efforts to free themselves, they could not sleep for wondering what the dawn would bring.

"Are you sure no one else followed you?" Jalair asked. "Then the Khan cares not that Iskander and I have left the city."

"As soon as the alarm was given," Dhuvik answered, "the Khan sent out parties of searchers. But they have ridden along the post roads and caravan trails and the hills beside them, for this is the only route Iskander would know. Yet I remembered that you came to Karakorum through the Takla Makan. Though I can not guess what hold this Iskander has over you to force you to release him, I knew he would make you avoid the trails. The Takla Makan is the only other route you knew of to take."

Dhuvik's loyalty shamed Jalair. "The desert is great, Dhuvik. How did you find us?"

"By the ringing of the Golden Hawks, whose flight makes them noticeable a great way off, as you know."

"It was daring, but foolish, to follow us alone," Jalair said. "Why did you not direct the searchers this way?"

Dhuvik was silent a moment. "They were angered by Iskander's escape, but the killing of the Golden Hawks outraged them beyond reason. Yatu spoke loud and convincingly, saying you were envious of his charge of the Goldens, and thus had released the goshawk which slaughtered them. I wanted to reach you first, lest anger make the searchers bare their swords before you could explain."

Jalair knew the truth would make Dhuvik his enemy. Yet he had chosen his path, and he could not use his friend's loyalty against him.

"But I wonder," Dhuvik continued, "what great bitterness made Iskander pause in his flight to kill the Golden Hawks. Did he think by this means to buy his way back into the graces of his Shah, bringing the last pair of Goldens?"

"Iskander had nothing to do with it," Jalair said, his heart heavy with the words he must speak if he would call himself honorable. "I did it myself."

There was a long silence.

"Then Yatu was right," Dhuvik said quietly. "Did Iskander by some means force you to rescue him?"

"No. It was all my own doing."

"Then why has Iskander bound you this night?"

"When I cried out your name, he heard in it my concern for you, and so tied me up in fear I could not be trusted."

"I see. You failed the trust we had in you, and Iskander fears you will fail his trust."

The words, though quietly spoken, were each an arrow in Jalair's heart. Not once had it occurred to him that he had betrayed Kaban's family and all the consideration with which the Mongols had treated him. Yet he was upholding an older loyalty as he sought to avenge Darien's death, Irian's enslavement, and the theft of the Golden Hawks.

"I am sorry that you have not been happy in Karakorum," Dhuvik added after a while.

"I have been happier there than at any time during my life!" Jalair cried, tears springing into his eyes. "I have never known father, mother, nor a brother such as you. I have never known a family such as yours has been to me, and gladly would I stay forever in the steppes of the Gobi!"

"Yet you fled," Dhuvik reminded him.

"When war was declared against Khoresm, I was greatly afraid. I did not want to be placed in a *kang*."

"You—in a *kang*?" Dhuvik was astonished. "But you are not a Khoresmian. You are a Mongol, and my father's second son. Did you not enter into the service of Genghis Khan, and wear the blue Hawker's cloak that made you a member of his court? Not as a Khoresmian, but only as a Mongol do one and all think of you!"

"I—I did not know this," Jalair said slowly. "But Iskander, a Khoresmian, was held prisoner."

"Iskander is a traitor to Shah Ala-u-Din," Dhuvik said.

"He told me otherwise."

"He lies."

Jalair did not wish to argue, and let the subject drop. Yet he cast about for some reason to explain his actions to Dhuvik. "Yatu hates me," he said. "I knew he would use the challenge of war in order to harm me, for all know that I envied his charge of the Golden Hawks and could not bear to see him fly them."

"Yatu's only concern is to safeguard the Golden Hawks until Torgul returns to take charge of them," Dhuvik said. After a moment, he added, "This love for the Goldens is more than a hawker's admiration for fine hawks. All summer, Jalair, I have seen a secret in your eyes. I did not speak, waiting instead for you to confide in me as a brother should. What is that secret? What made you come to Karakorum?"

"In Samarkand I had been told many stories about Mongols—of their treachery and cruelty. I believed them, but now I know that much I heard is not true." He did not add that one tale of cruelty Torgul could not deny.

"Then, as you have already learned that Mongols can be men of honor and trust, will you not tell me this terrible secret you hold? Surely it is something I can explain!"

But Jalair could say no more. It might be that he would

let be captured by Genghis Khan's searchers. And at all costs, they must not learn that he was Darien's son.

"Trust me, Dhuvik, when I say my reason is a good one. Perhaps I acted foolishly, yet my feet are set upon the path I have taken, and there is no turning back. Though it was fear that drove me, still I did release Iskander. I did steal a pair of the Golden Hawks, and I caused the slaughter of the hawks that remained. These deeds cannot be changed."

In spite of all the things that had happened, and in spite of his change of heart, Jalair fixed his mind on the single goal that had taken him to the land of Genghis Khan, and was now leading him back to Khoresm.

One Golden Hawk remained.

Perhaps he could yet salvage the strain.

Dawn crept across the waste of sands, but Jalair did not see the growing morning until Iskander kicked him awake. The courtier cut his bonds and pushed him toward Dhuvik's supplies, piled near the previous night's fire, with the command to make breakfast.

Jalair did the work quickly, and Iskander allowed him to eat also. "May I feed Empress?" Jalair asked when they had finished the meal.

"After you have packed all supplies on the horse," Iskander said. "The weapons also," he added, gesturing to the pile of arms beside his bedding. "Remember, I will be watching."

And watch Iskander did, with eyes rivaled only by the keen sight of the Golden Hawk. Jalair had no chance to slip any edged object—knife or arrow—inside his jacket. As he tied the last of the equipment behind Dhuvik's saddle, he was greatly tempted to leap upon the horse and gallop off. Yet Dhuvik was still tightly trussed up, and Jalair could not leave him to face Iskander's fury. Most important of all, the Golden Hawk must not be left behind either.

Dhuvik was awake by now, shifting restlessly to ease his aching limbs. Jalair glanced at him with concern.

"He will be fed later in the day," Iskander growled. "We have little time, for men may have followed him."

"You promised I could feed Empress."

"Then hurry."

Jalair had put a handful of Dhuvik's trail rations inside his jacket, and now he went to the ledge where Empress had spent the night. He put on the leather gauntlet and coaxed Empress upon his fist, grasping her leash between his fingers. Then he unhooded her with his free hand, and fed her bits of meat. She ate greedily, and soon finished the store of food Jalair had taken for her.

"Jalair, turn around!"

Iskander had been standing close while Jalair fed Empress, and he had just stepped up behind him. The command came suddenly, and Jalair turned, Empress still on his fist.

The rising sun winked on a cold steel blade that flashed forth in Iskander's hand. The gleaming point was held near the breast of the last Golden Hawk. "Do not move," Iskander grated. "Or the falcon will die."

Jalair looked into Iskander's dark eyes, and his mouth went dry as he wondered what mad plan the courtier was carrying out.

"Your friendship with our captive makes me uneasy," Iskander said, still keeping the knife close to the Golden's breast while Jalair stood rigid with fear. "For this reason, I need your promise to help me." He smiled. "I am told you keep your word."

"Yes." Jalair spoke absently, fascinated by the gleaming knife that hovered so close to Empress' golden breast. He wanted to fling his arm up, casting the falcon away from the sharp blade. But he knew that Iskander's knife would be there first.

"This Mongol boy—Dhuvik, you said his name is," Iskander said. "We can take him with us to Shah Ala-u-Din. He is of the age to be trained for the army, and he can be made to tell the Shah of Genghis Khan's troops and their methods of attack. The Shah will reward us richly for that information, and even give us places of honor in his court."

Jalair glanced swiftly at Dhuvik, whose study of Turki throughout the summer enabled him to follow the conversation. From his friend's set jaw and flashing eyes, Jalair knew

Dhuvik would never voluntarily reveal any information for Shah Ala-u-Din.

"He knows nothing," Jalair answered. "His father is but a leader of caravans, and his son is trained only for that task. He has no interest in military matters."

"Why, Jalair, you know better than that." Iskander grinned. "For many years the Shah has kept close watch on the growing empire of Genghis Khan, lest the Mongol become too powerful for Khoresmian liking. It is known that all boys of our captive's age either attend the officers' school, or enter the ranks. His helmet has the red horsetail crest, which marks him as a cadet officer."

Iskander waited a moment, and then his tongue grew cunning. "Do not think this captive is any friend of yours. Released, he would gallop to the Mongols who surely are searching for us. Now think of this, Jalair. The Shah would welcome us if we brought back a Mongol captive who could be made to reveal many secrets."

"The Shah will give us welcome enough when I return with the Golden Hawk and perhaps salvage the great strain," Jalair countered.

Iskander's harsh laugh startled Empress who shifted her feet on Jalair's fist. "You would insult the Shah with your precious falcon!" Iskander cried. "He would have it destroyed at once—unless," and his voice became honeyed with persuasion, "unless we bring a captive to temper the Shah's wrath."

"Are you afraid to return to Urgendj without a hostage?" Jalair cried angrily.

"It is for you to fear to approach the Shah without your friend as hostage!" Iskander exulted, the knife wavering dangerously close to the Golden falcon. He breathed heavily as one rejoicing in unaccustomed power. "Know this, Jalair. You will find no welcome at Urgendj unless you deliver your friend to the Shah. Perhaps then—" his voice smoothed craftily, "—then you can keep your Golden falcon. I will speak for you, and you will be allowed to study hawking."

Jalair knew the bargain could be made and would be

honored. It was a small price for Shah Ala-u-Din to pay for any secrets he might wring from Dhuvik.

Though in this matter Iskander spoke the truth, Jalair knew he had lied often before. All the little clues Jalair had pushed away came swirling to the surface.

Iskander spoke only Turki and Arabic. His prison guards knew only the Mongol tongue. Yet Iskander had said the guards questioned him continually in the prison *yurt*. Then after Jalair had discussed the escape, Iskander had not confided his plan for leaving the prison *yurt* until after they had met on the plain. Too clearly, he remembered Iskander's sudden fright when he thought Jalair might lead him into a Mongol trap. If Iskander could not trust Jalair, then he himself could not be trusted.

And because Kurush had taught him that all Mongols were thieves and murderers, Jalair had been ready to believe anything Iskander might say against them.

Jalair stared into Iskander's insolent eyes, and knew him for a traitor.

"What enraged the Shah against you that you must flee to Genghis Khan with your offer of treachery?" Jalair asked boldly.

"I could not return to Urgendj without you," Iskander replied, now casting off all pretense of loyalty. "I feared the Shah would cast me into prison, and so I escaped along the caravan route." He smiled. "Though Genghis Khan disappointed me with his honorable principles, I had the luck to find you, and realized I could yet redeem my position with the Shah. And our captive will insure our welcome, for I think your stay in Karakorum will displease the Shah greatly."

"What has Shah Ala-u-Din to do with me?" Jalair demanded. "Why would he imprison you for failing to bring me to Urgendj?"

Iskander's silence mocked him.

"If you let Dhuvik go," Jalair bargained, "I will return of my own free will. If not, I will tell the Shah you are a traitor."

"And of course," Iskander smiled, "the Shah would believe you."

And Jalair knew he was defeated.

If he made the promise Iskander demanded, he would have to keep it. From the personal courage and honor of the Mongols had sprung the strict code of the *Yassa*. Dhuvik would refuse to escape under a lie.

"I hold the knife, Jalair," Iskander warned him. "It is I who make the bargain. In exchange for your promise to return with me and not attempt Dhuvik's release, I give you the Golden falcon and a chance for you to salvage the strain. If you do not give me that promise, one thrust of my hand will forever end what I heard you call the greatest hawk strain in the world."

The long search for the Golden Hawks, born of a dream

and a promise to the memory of Darien, had brought Jalair to the midst of this vast desert where the thrust of a man's hand could end forever the magnificent strain.

He remembered what he had thought beneath the stars of the long night when he lay bound beside Dhuvik. At all costs, the last Golden Hawk must be saved. For without it, there would be no Darien to cling to, even in his dreams. Without it there would be neither purpose nor hope to help him bear the bitter consequences awaiting him in both Urgendj and Karakorum.

His struggle must have been mirrored on his face, for Iskander laughed. "Decide now, Jalair. Or the falcon will die."

"I have decided," Jalair sighed, his voice heavy with sorrow.

Iskander's lips twisted into a smile, and he relaxed, letting the knife drop a little.

Jalair snapped his wrist. "Fly, Empress!" he cried.

He felt the great wind coming from the Golden Hawk's wings as Empress flung herself from his fist, claws foremost. A blinding sparkle of gold feathers dazzled him as the falcon bolted into Iskander's face.

A terrified scream echoed and re-echoed across the desert, and through it the dull thud of arms striking the falcon.

Empress struggled and beat her wings furiously, and then a fist shot out, striking the fighting bundle of golden feathers to the ground.

The last Golden Hawk twitched weakly, then lay still in the sands.

For an instant Jalair saw Iskander's face before the man pressed his hands to it. His forehead and cheeks were slashed and blood flowed into his eyes, temporarily blinding him. Iskander blotted his sleeve against the wounds, but could not staunch the flow.

"Jalair, Jalair!" he cried. "Where are you? Bring me water!"

But the memory of a golden breast stained with blood hardened Jalair's heart, and he neither moved nor answered.

Iskander reeled, his foot striking the bloody knife he had dropped. "Jalair, help me! Wash my eyes. I can not see!"

Iskander's voice echoed through the wasteland. He staggered to find the horse with its supplies and water flasks, but in his confusion he wandered out past the rock outcrop where they had made camp.

"I promise, Jalair, I promise!" Iskander shouted as he took his hands from his bleeding face and flailed the air with his arms. "Help me, and I will release Dhuvik. And you too!"

But no traitor keeps his promises, and Jalair stood silent, as though rooted to the ground, for the slightest shift of sand beneath his feet would give Iskander his position.

Iskander's voice was growing fainter as he wandered dizzily into the desert. He coaxed, he promised, he shouted and threatened, and he staggered farther away.

Was it an hour, two hours? Jalair did not know. For a long time now Iskander had been out of sight beyond the sand dunes, and even the breeze did not carry back his words.

At last Jalair dared move.

He picked up Iskander's knife, the knife that had forever ended all Darien's work, and going to Dhuvik he cut his friend's bonds.

Neither boy spoke, but there was a wonder and an admiration in Dhuvik's eyes as he rubbed his sore wrists and walked beside Jalair.

They stood over the Golden Hawk, the great hunter of the skies that had died such an ignoble death upon the desert sands.

Jalair knelt and took the limp falcon in his hands, feeling the sleek stiffness of the golden feathers that once flashed dauntlessly in the sun.

He bowed his head, and began to weep.

15 Torgul Returns

Dhuvik's hand fell on Jalair's shoulder, and there was no need for words.

Then Dhuvik unpicketed his horse and led it to Jalair who still crouched on the sands. Jalair gently laid the Golden Hawk on the ground, then turned away with sagging shoulders and climbed into the saddle.

Dhuvik put his foot into the stirrup, then hesitated. "Will you take the body of the falcon?"

Jalair shook his head. "No. Let it, in death, be free from the hand of a master."

Dhuvik mounted in front of his friend and turned to the north.

"Are you not going to search for Iskander?" Jalair asked.

"To what end?" Dhuvik countered. "My supplies now will last the two of us on horseback only to the nearest post station. If we captured Iskander, we would be reduced to a footpace." A little later he added, "Turfan is only three days away. We can send men after Iskander."

For three days they pushed on as rapidly as they could to Turfan. Though the horse traveled more slowly under its double burden, the boys made up the distance by taking only three or four hours for sleep late at night. They spoke little, their ears filled with the drumming sands and each sunk in his own thoughts.

Only once during the entire trip north did they refer to the terrible crisis near the rock outcropping.

"You could have accepted Iskander's bargain," Dhuvik said.

"I could not turn against my brother, the only friend I have ever had."

"You know you must answer for your deeds when we return," Dhuvik reminded him. "There is yet a chance for you to escape, though in all honor I cannot help you do this."

"No," Jalair said quietly. "I made my decision when I sacrificed the Golden Hawk. I cannot live except in the steppes and the mountains. Even if it be as a prisoner, my heart will still know the freedom of the winds across the plains, and I will yet hear the wild horsemen shout as they gallop beneath the hawks."

"And the terrible secret in your heart? Will it not embitter you against these great plains you say you love?"

Jalair sighed wearily, and he thought of Darien.

"I find my loyalty to Kaban's family and the people of the steppes is greater than a dream I once had," he said slowly. It is fine to revere a memory, dim though it be. Yet the world is here and now. It must be lived in, and each man must decide upon his own loyalties.

The buildings of Turfan rose up from the desert on the evening of their third day of travel. Turfan, a caravan stopover, had become for Jalair the beginning and the end of a strange conflict of loyalties. Here, Kaban had sent the carved horn to Genghis Khan. And here, Jalair was returning of his own will to Genghis Khan's judgment. Though he had found his place in the world a little too late, still he had found it.

They jogged on steadily to the post station beside the caravan trail on the outskirts of the city.

As soon as their tired mount was turned into the corral and the boys told of their journey, two messengers on fast horses galloped out to contact the nearest search party. Another group of men rode south, leading an extra horse in case they should succeed in finding Iskander.

The boys were fed, for they had gone hungry since their supplies gave out that morning. Then they dropped to straw pallets and fell asleep.

The next afternoon the searchers arrived, a grim party of Mongols led by a man Jalair recognized, but whose name he could not recall. Dhuvik quickly sketched in the events in the desert, then two horses were saddled for the boys.

As Jalair mounted, he turned to the officer, concealing as well as he could the sudden stab of fear he felt at returning to Karakorum. "What will happen to me?"

"We have no orders, except to return with you," the officer replied, then gave the order to start.

At least, Jalair thought as he kicked his horse into a canter, no one knew he was Darien's son.

The return to Karakorum was a speedy one, for at every

post station along the way the group changed to fresh horses and pushed on. Nor did they stop even for a little sleep, but dozed now and then in rocking saddles as the horses galloped along.

They were joined by a messenger, exhausted from his terrible ride from Turfan. Jalair caught Iskander's name as the messenger panted his news to the officer, while the group rode on without slacking pace. He turned to Dhuvik riding beside him. "Did they kill Iskander?"

"No need," Dhuvik said. "He had gone five days without water."

Jalair knew that even three waterless days could be fatal.

They were but a day's forced ride from Karakorum when, in the flat light of dawn, they saw a distant horseman galloping toward them. A messenger from Karakorum, Jalair thought, and he dreaded the order the man might bring.

The search party never slackened its pace, and so they soon met with the horseman speeding toward them. When the rider pulled his reins, making his horse rear and prance, Jalair saw that it was Yatu!

He was shouting something, and the words chilled Jalair to the marrow.

For Yatu cried, "Where is Darien's son?"

The red flames of the thorn fire leaped about the armor hanging on the curved felt walls of Kaban's *yurt*. It was very late at night, and the search party had arrived at Karakorum not an hour before. Yatu had then taken charge of Jalair, escorting him and Dhuvik to the *yurt* where Kaban greeted them.

Chentai made them all sit down at once and begin the meal that had been laid out for them. Jalair had little appetite, so heavy was the fear Yatu had awakened when he called him Darien's son. Nor had Yatu explained, merely saying as they galloped on to the city, "It is Kaban's story, and he it is who will tell it." Dhuvik's startled expression had shown that he knew nothing of this new development.

After the late meal, Yatu departed, saying he had business with the Khan.

"Well, Jalair," said Kaban. He seemed uncertain how to begin.

Jalair could not face his steady gaze. "I stole your horses, saddles, and supplies."

"That does not matter, for everything in this household is equally shared by all," Kaban said.

"Well, I did things which betrayed you and the Khan," Jalair said. "Do with me what you will." But whatever should happen, Jalair was determined not to plead or protest. For these were "the Brave People," and he resolved to be one of them. "Besides," Jalair added, "now you know Darien was my father."

"Then it's really true, Father?" Dhuvik exclaimed. "Is Jalair really Darien's son?"

"True indeed," Kaban said, and he turned to Jalair. "I first suspected you were Darien's son when I saw the design you carved on the horn for Dhuvik. I recognized the hawk riding a thunderbolt. Yet you could have seen the design and still not be Darien's son. I found the truth when last I was in Samarkand." Kaban's glance included Chentai and Dhuvik, for they had not yet heard the story. "It is a tale of which Jalair knows little. It began many years ago, in the court of Samarkand's governor. Kurush, the city Treasurer's Steward, planned to increase his chances of promotion by marrying his daughter Irian to the son of Urgendj's governor.

"But Irian was in love with the Hawker to Shah Ala-u-Din. He was Darien—strong, handsome, and clever. Kurush did not approve of the union, and so they ran off together and married secretly. Knowing the enraged Kurush would have soldiers searching for them, they traveled to Karakorum where Darien offered his services to Genghis Khan. They were both happy in the city, Irian with the son born to them here in the steppes, and Darien with developing the greatest hawk the world has seen—the Golden Hawk—in honor of Genghis Khan."

Jalair could hardly absorb so much at once. "I was born here—in Karakorum?"

"In a *yurt* that was Darien's, near the mews of the Golden Hawks," Kaban said.

And the Golden Hawks were in honor of Genghis Khan —not Shah Ala-u-Din! No wonder Iskander said Jalair's "gift" would be an insult to the Shah.

"Not only was Darien the Khan's Hawker," Kaban continued, "but his talent for diplomacy and scholarship brought him to a high position in the Khan's court. In the Year of the Panther, when Jalair was only four years of age, Cathay began marauding forays against the tribes north of the Great Wall. Since these tribes were allies of Genghis Khan, they appealed to him for help. The Khan sent Darien to the Cathayan court to settle the dispute."

Kaban paused to refresh himself from the horn of rice wine he held. "While Darien was in Cathay, Irian was traveling back to Samarkand with Jalair. Though she planned to live always in Karakorum, the thought of her father's disapproval and anger made her unhappy. She thought to soften his heart by showing him his grandchild. But in Samarkand, Kurush refused to see her. A fever, contracted on the journey, had weakened Irian so she could not return with her escort of the Khan's warriors. She settled in a little house in Samarkand with her child, planning to return to Karakorum when her health had mended.

"Only a month had passed since the escort returned when word came of Darien. Instead of treating him as an envoy of Genghis Khan, the Cathayans had thrown him into prison and questioned him about the Khan's military secrets, for they were afraid of the rising Mongol empire. Darien smuggled out word of his predicament, but before he could be rescued, the Cathayans executed him in a rage over his refusal to betray the Khan. At once the Khan marshaled his huge army, and soon marched through the Great Wall."

"Then my father died a hero's death, instead of being struck down ignobly as Kurush told me!" Jalair exclaimed. Now Darien's death could be a source of pride instead of fear.

"Genghis Khan at once sent a group of men to bring Irian and Darien's son back to Karakorum. I was a member of that group. When we came to Irian's house in Samarkand, servants told us that she had died of the fever only two weeks before. They had sent word of her death to Kurush, who came and took her child into his house. We then went to the house of Kurush and told him of Darien's death, saying we must return at once with his son. Kurush made many excuses, saying the boy still grieved over his mother's death, and that he was too young for the long journey."

Jalair pondered, trying to remember Irian's home in Samarkand, but all he could call up were the large halls of Kurush's grand house. Yet he had memories, for out of his early life had come the vision of the secret land, the longing for hawks, and the picture of a man and a woman that Chentai's singing always conjured up.

"We had to return without Darien's son," Kaban continued. "Six months later, Genghis Khan sent us again with a sharply worded note to Kurush, demanding the child's return. Again Kurush delayed, saying it would be better if he educated the boy in Samarkand's schools. He promised to send him to the Khan when he was fifteen years of age. Once more we returned empty-handed. As Khoresm was a strongly guarded empire, and the Khan was occupied with the conquest, and then the governing of Cathay, there was nothing to do but wait.

"Years later, on a caravan trail, I saw this design carved on a drinking horn." Kaban paused while he took from his belt a copper disk hung on a beaten copper chain and handed it to Jalair.

The boy held it to catch the light of the burning thorns. In low relief on the copper disk was the plunging hawk and the thunderbolt beneath. Jalair touched the polished surface and a wave of remembrance broke over him. "This is mine," he said. "I cannot remember ever actually seeing it before, but I know it is mine."

"And so it is, from the hand of Genghis Khan." Kaban smiled. "He placed this gift around your neck when you were born, and everyone knew how fond of it you were for you wore it always."

"But where did you find it?" Jalair cried in amazement.

"Kurush took it from you and hid it," Kaban answered.

"One thing I do not understand," Jalair said. "If Kurush would not come to my mother when she was ill, why did he take me into his house?"

"There is much we do not know," Kaban admitted. "Yet it is easy to read the mind of a selfish, grasping man, hungry for a high position. Kurush had already made arrangements for Irian to marry the son of Urgendj's governor. Therefore, when Irian ran off with Darien, Kurush must have suffered the anger of the governor, who is said to have great influence with Shah Ala-u-Din since his court is in Urgendj. When Irian communicated with Kurush, she undoubtedly informed him of Darien's important position with Genghis Khan in an effort to make her father proud of her husband. Having learned of Darien's death, Kurush must have realized how anxious Genghis Khan was to have the child sent back to Karakorum.

"Certainly it was known to all court officials that we Mongols would soon grow into a great power. Perhaps Kurush thought to turn you into a spy for Shah Ala-u-Din when you would be sent back to us. Or he might have thought to use you as a hostage, letting the Shah bargain your return for certain concessions from the Khan. In either case, he saw in you an opportunity for regaining his lost prestige and of advancing to a high post."

"Kurush curried favor among the courtiers of Samarkand's governor," Jalair said. "Iskander said he fled from Shah Ala-u-Din's anger when I ran away from Samarkand. That was the night before I was to go to Urgendj with him."

Jalair remembered other things. Kurush's anger at the hawk design Jalair always drew or carved. His disapproval of hawking, for it reminded him of the man who had caused him humiliation. Jalair being sent away to school in a small village where no one could tell him of his past. Trusted Cephas, always at his side. The Mongols in Samarkand, and Kurush's warnings. And the tales Kurush told—of vicious Mongols cutting down his father, enslaving his mother, and stealing the Golden Hawks. Stories designed to turn Jalair forever against the people with whom his father had chosen to make his home. But Kurush had gone too far in creating Jalair's hatred.

He should never have mentioned the Golden Hawks.

Tears started in Jalair's eyes. The Golden Hawks had been needlessly sacrificed.

"Then this is the secret you kept all summer," Dhuvik said. "That Darien was your father. But why?"

Jalair nodded. "I feared you would kill me, for that is what I had been told." He explained, then, what Kurush had repeated so often to build Jalair's fear and hatred of the Mongols. And he told of Iskander, the stranger from Urgendj, whose coming had sent Jalair out on the caravan trails to the land of Genghis Khan.

When he fell silent, Dhuvik began telling in detail of the crisis in the Takla Makan and how Jalair had met the challenge.

Throughout, Kaban had not moved except to throw more thorns on the dying fire.

Jalair broke his silence when Dhuvik finished his tale. "If only I had known all this! I would not have envied Yatu the Golden Hawks. Or if only I had told Dhuvik my secret, he could have explained. Now—" He glanced at the copper talisman, at the hawk and the thunderbolt, and thought of the great days when he and Idikut galloped beneath the hawks. "Now I have betrayed not only my family, but also my real father."

"It was not betrayal," said a deep voice.

Jalair glanced at the doorway of the *yurt* where Yatu and Genghis Khan had been standing quietly in the shadows as the boys told their stories.

It was Genghis Khan who had spoken, and now he entered, Yatu behind him. Everyone rose at once and did not sit down until the Khan had been seated on an embroidered cushion at the place of honor opposite the doorway.

"It is fitting that I come to Darien's son," said the Khan, explaining the unusual visit. He took the horn of rice wine Kaban handed him. "Dhuvik may now drink from the horn Jalair carved for him." From his wide belt he took the carved drinking horn and handed it to Kaban's son. Everyone looked from the horn to the copper talisman Jalair had put around his neck, and the designs matched in every detail.

"It was not betrayal," the Khan continued, turning to Jalair, "but a conflict of loyalties. Your first duty was to the memory of your father, Darien, even if that memory was based on falsehood. Yet, by living among us, you attained some allegiance to what you considered Darien's enemies. When war was declared on Khoresm, you had to choose between these loyalties. I know now the fears that caused your flight from Karakorum.

"In the Takla Makan, Iskander forced a second choice, but now the answer involved more than your personal desires. Because of that, you chose to be loyal to the people among whom you had lived and worked. And for them you sacrificed the Golden Hawk."

Jalair shuddered, remembering that terrible decision in the desert.

"Little harm was done," the Khan said. "Tomorrow, you may rest. But on the day after, I think there is work waiting for you in the mews."

"Then I am not to be punished?" Jalair asked incredulously.

The Khan smiled through his fiery beard. "I think the years of unhappiness with Kurush are punishment enough, as was the agony of two decisions." He turned to Kaban. "Has Jalair heard how you discovered his past?"

"Not all of the story, my Khan," Kaban replied. "The carved design interested me. Yet the talisman could have been lost, then found by someone else. Or someone could have shown you the design, if not the talisman itself. I could not speak these thoughts until I knew the real answers. After all, Jalair, it was entirely possible you were a spy for Shah Ala-u-Din."

"Well, so we suspected each other of trickery all along!" Jalair laughed, feeling a little better.

"I also noted your interest in hawking." Kaban smiled. "And you had told me you were an orphan. All this I reported to the Khan when we arrived in Karakorum. Meanwhile I had sent the carved horn ahead."

"For what purpose?" Jalair asked.

"To keep it from being seen by anyone other than the Khan," Kaban explained. "The design is easily recognized by almost every warrior in Karakorum, and there was certain to be talk of Darien and his missing son. The Khan also forbade anyone to discuss Darien and his deeds. Otherwise, if you were a spy, it would have been easy for you to play the part of Darien's son according to what you heard."

"Still, Jalair," Genghis Khan said, "it was with no thought that you might be Darien's son that I allowed you to work with Idikut. Anyone choosing to dwell in my empire may do the work for which he is best suited."

"And you would still live with us, Jalair," Dhuvik added. "When you joined the caravan, you said you wished to go to Karakorum. Father and I talked of taking you into our family long before you carved the horn."

"True enough," Kaban agreed. "No matter who you were, you would always be welcome in my *yurt*. Yet we saw these clues to your background, and the Khan ordered me to discover whether you were really Darien's son when next I went to Samarkand. Before I could look into the matter, Inaldjuk seized the caravan at Otrar, and I was otherwise occupied for a while."

"Occupied!" cried Dhuvik, remembering Kaban's protest to Shah Ala-u-Din and his escape from Khoresm's soldiers. "I should say you were!"

Kaban laughed, and continued his story. "After I refused the Shah's hospitality and did other necessary tasks, I lingered in Samarkand with three of my men. We went to the house of Kurush, and found him gone. He had taken two servants with him, leaving the rest to pack his goods and bring them to Baghdad."

"Was Cephas left behind?" Jalair could not help but ask. "He was kind to me, and shielded me from Kurush's anger."

"No one was there of that name," Kaban replied. "I questioned the servants, showing them the point of my sword, and they answered readily."

"You are not as diplomatic as Darien," Genghis Khan said with a grin almost concealed by his red beard.

"My Khan, there was little time and the streets were thick with soldiers looking for me. Indeed, we would have been caught at once had we not borrowed robes such as the men of Khoresm wear."

"Kurush's servants knew nothing of my past, I am certain," Jalair said. "Kurush trusted no one."

"But they showed me the things Kurush left behind in

his secret hiding place," Kaban grinned. "I knew your birth could be proved by the talisman you are now wearing around your neck. Kurush's plans would be useless unless he could produce the talisman for the Shah—who also trusts no one. Besides the talisman, I found the letter our Khan had sent Kurush years ago, demanding your return."

"Why did he leave these things behind?" Jalair wondered. "They expose the secret he was keeping."

"Because the secret was no longer of any use to him," Kaban replied. "The servants said that as soon as Kurush heard of the incident at Otrar, he fled to Baghdad. He knew how strong the Khan's troops are, and war was inevitable. He feared the Khan's anger toward him when Samarkand should be taken."

"Did he know I went to Karakorum?" Jalair asked.

"No one knew that," Kaban said. "Kurush only thought you ran away so you would not be sent to Urgendj. And he had no liking for helping to defend Khoresm. The servants told me that the Shah was greatly angered when Jalair left the house of Kurush."

"Your journey east has done many things." Dhuvik grinned. "It made you find the truth about your father. It made Kurush flee from Samarkand. And it made Iskander turn traitor."

"It also caused the destruction of the Golden Hawks," Jalair added quietly.

Genghis Khan gestured to Yatu, who rose and stepped outside. He came back, gently carrying a basket which he set before Jalair.

"Open it, Jalair," the Khan urged.

Jalair threw back the lid of the basket. By the leaping firelight he could see six balls of golden feathers. They tumbled about in the basket, trying to climb over the side.

"Three pairs of Golden Hawks," the Khan said. "All that are left."

"These fledglings were in Idikut's *yurt*," Yatu explained. "The better that he could care for them while they are so young."

"Now they are for you to care for," Genghis Khan said. "Raise them well."

"Me?" Jalair raised his head. "You would trust me with them?"

"I was only to care for them until their true master returned," Yatu smiled.

"But Torgul is their master!"

"Torgul is your real name," Kaban explained gently. "Kurush changed it—partly to keep you ignorant of your past, and partly because it reminded him of Darien's joining Genghis Khan's court."

So that was why the name nagged Jalair with maddening familiarity! It is not easy to make someone forget his own name, though Kurush nearly succeeded.

"Torgul has returned," said Yatu with a grin of satisfaction. "The Golden Hawks are in his care, and an old pledge has been kept."

Through the long cold winter as the wind whined on the steppes, and smoke holes were closed against the raging blizzards, Jalair learned to answer to his real name, Torgul. While hardened warriors massed and went off to Khoresm, their faces smeared with grease against the cutting cold, his fingers learned gentleness as he handled the young Golden Hawks, and became indifferent to their hardening claws and sharp beaks. The herds on the plains grew lean, and their ranks thinned as the hungry winter wore on. But inside the mews of the Golden Hawks, Torgul carefully fed the young birds to bring the sleek stiffness to their flight feathers that made them the most powerful hawks ever known.

And then one day the sun stayed in the sky for a long time, unhindered by clouds, and the snows began to melt. Soon the earth was rich and black and wet, and then began to turn green. The smell of spring invaded the mews of the Goldens, and the hawks' young master knew it was time to stretch their wings.

And so it was that a boy on a horse, carrying a pair of fierce-eyed hawks whose feathers caught the dawning sun, rode out on the plains surrounding Karakorum.

He threw the first from his fist, and the Golden Hawk sprang up to the sky for which he had been born, and stroked his mighty golden wings with a passion and a hunger.

The hawk ringed and ringed until it was a tiny yellow dot. Then the spark of gold grew larger as the hawk plummeted earthward, wings folded against its body.

Faster and faster the Golden Hawk plunged toward the ground, the sun seeming to strike sparks from its feathers.

And truly, it did seem to be riding a thunderbolt.

Bibliography

FALCONRY

Brooks, Maj. Allan. "Eagles, Hawks, and Vultures," *National Geographic Magazine*, Vol. LXIV, No. 1, July, 1933.

Craighead, Frank and John. "Adventures with Birds of Prey," *National Geographic Magazine*, Vol. LXXII, No. 1, July, 1937.

———. "Life with an Indian Prince," *National Geographic Magazine*, Vol. LXXXI, No. 2, February, 1942.

Fuertes, Louis Agassiz. "Falconry, the Sport of Kings," *National Geographic Magazine*, Vol. XXXVIII, No. 6, December, 1920.

———. "American Birds of Prey, A Review of Their Value," *National Geographic Magazine*, Vol. XXXVIII, No. 6, December, 1920.

Wetmore, Alexander. "The Eagle, King of Birds, and His Kin," *National Geographic Magazine*, Vol. LXIV, No. 1, July, 1933.

Wood, Casey A., and Fyfe, F. Marjorie, editors and translators. *The Art of Falconry, being the De Arte Venandi Cum Avibus of Frederick II of Hohenstaufen*, Stanford University Press, Stanford, California, 1943.

ASIA FROM WEST TO EAST

Hildebrand, J. R. "The World's Greatest Overland Explorer," *National Geographic Magazine*, Vol. LIV, No. 5, November, 1928.

Iacovleff, Alexandre. "Faces and Fashions of Asia's Changeless Tribes," *National Geographic Magazine*, Vol. LXIX, No. 1, January, 1936.

Williams, Maynard Owen. "From the Mediterranean to the Yellow Sea by Motor," "Bright Pages from an Asiatic Travel Log," "The Land of Genghis Khan in Its True Colors,"

National Geographic Magazine, Vol. LXII, No. 5, November, 1932.

THE MONGOLS

Andrews, Roy Chapman. "Explorations in the Gobi Desert," "Nomad Life and Fossil Treasures of Mongolia," *National Geographic Magazine*, Vol. LXII, No. 6, June, 1933.

Bretschneider, E., M.D., editor and translator. *Mediaeval Researches from Eastern Asiatic Sources; Fragments Towards the Knowledge of the Geography and History of Central and Western Asia from the Thirteenth to the Seventeenth Century*, Vol. I, K. Paul, Trench, Trubner & Co., Ltd., London, 1888.

Komroff, Manuel, editor. *Contemporaries of Marco Polo, consisting of the travel records to the eastern parts of the world of William of Rubruck (1253-1255); the journey of John of Pian de Carpini (1245-1247); the journal of Friar Odoric (1318-1330); and the oriental travels of Rabbi Benjamin of Tudela (1160-1173)*; Liveright Pub. Corp., New York, 1928.

Murray, Edward. "With the Nomads of Central Asia," *National Geographic Magazine*, Vol. LXIX, No. 1, January, 1936.

THE KHORESMIANS

Gibb, Hamilton A. R. *Mohammedanism, An Historical Survey*, (2nd ed.) Oxford University Press, New York, 1953.

Larned, J. N. *Seventy Centuries of the Life of Mankind*, Vol. I, C. A. Nichols Pub. Co., Springfield, Massachusetts, 1905.

Malcolm, Sir John. *The History of Persia from the Most Early Period to the Present Time*, Vol. I, John Murray, Ltd., London, 1829.

Sykes, Sir Percy. *A History of Persia*, (3rd ed.), Vol. II, Macmillan & Co., Ltd., London, 1951.

Wilbur, Lyman D. "Surveying Through Koresm," *National Geographic Magazine*, Vol. LXI, No. 6, June, 1932.

CPSIA information can be obtained
at www.ICGtesting.com
Printed in the USA
BVHW072026010719
552308BV00007B/270/P